THE QuestKids®

Coding with HTML & JavaScript

Create Epic Computer Games

=y+3;

y=y+2;

canvas

src='plane.png'

height:90px;

<img>

y=y+1;

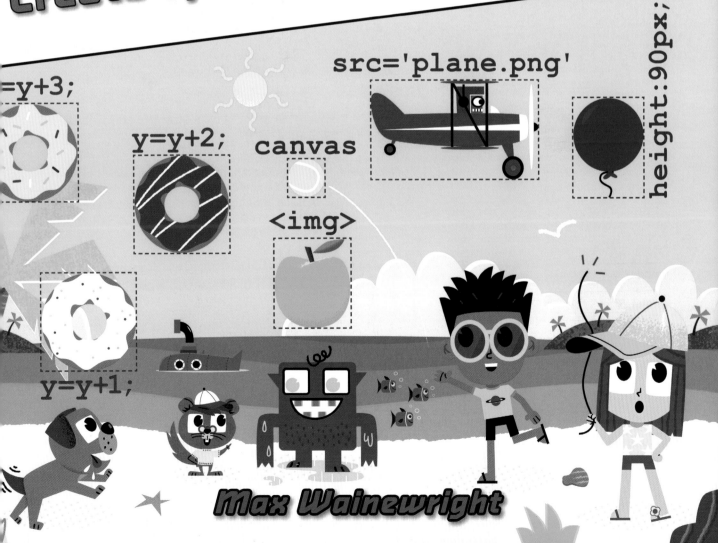

Max Wainewright

To create the games in this book you will need:

- a computer or laptop with a proper keyboard – an iPad or any other tablet will not work so well.

- an internet connection to download resources used in the book.

It is recommended that children should be supervised when using the internet, especially when using a new website. The publishers and the author cannot be held responsible for the content of the websites referred to in this book.

For further help and resources with this book, visit www.maxw.com or thequestkids.com

The QuestKids® series is an imprint of In Easy Steps Limited
16 Hamilton Terrace, Holly Walk, Leamington Spa,
Warwickshire, United Kingdom CV32 4LY
www.ineasysteps.com
www.thequestkids.com

ISBN: 978-1-84078-955-3

MIX
Paper from
responsible sources
FSC® C020837

Printed and bound in the United Kingdom

Notice of Liability
Every effort has been made to ensure that this book contains accurate and current information. However, In Easy Steps Limited and the authors shall not be liable for any loss or damage suffered by readers as a result of any information contained herein.

Contributors:
Author: Max Wainewright
Creative Designer: Jo Cowan
Cover & character illustrations: Marcelo (The Bright Agency)

Acknowledgements
The publisher would like to thank the following sources for the use of their background illustrations:

Dreamstime, iStock, Shutterstock.com

Contents

Getting Started

In this book you will learn how to create your own games using HTML and JavaScript. These are some of the coding languages used by professional game developers.

We will begin by getting images to move and making code run when they are clicked. Later, we'll find out how to control things with keyboard presses and how to run code repeatedly with timers. Variables will let us keep track of where things are and how many points players score. You'll learn how to import images and add sounds to bring your games to life!

Score: 17

Score: 5

Develop your skills and build some amazing games!

1 Find a text editor

You need a program called a text editor to type in your code. You may have one on your computer. If not then ask someone if you can download one.

www.sublimetext.com

Open your web browser and go to

www.sublimetext.com

We recommend Sublime Text, which is free to use.

2 Download it

Click the **DOWNLOAD** button at the top of the page.

xt Editing, Done Rig

DOWNLOAD

Wait while the file downloads.

3 Run the download

Double-click the downloaded file to start installing the software.

sublime_text_buil....

4 Install the download

The software should now start to install on your computer.

Installing

Sublime Text

Follow any steps shown on screen to get your text editor installed.

HTML stands for HyperText Markup Language.

HTML was designed as a way of creating and linking together pages of information around the world. The first version of HTML was coded by Tim Berners-Lee.

Saying Hello

1 Start a new HTML file

 Open your text editor.

2 Save your file

Click **File > Save**.

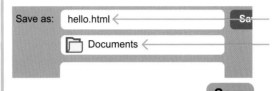

Type in **hello.html** as the file name.

Browse to your Documents folder.

Click **Save**.

3 Start coding

Type the first line of code.

```
1 <html>
```

Hold down the **Shift** key...

...and press these keys to get the symbols you need:

*In HTML these are usually called **angle brackets**.*

The colours change automatically to help you read your code.

4 Finish the code

Finish typing the code.

```
1 <html>
2     <h1>Hello</h1>
3 </html>
```

Start of the HTML.
Add a heading that says Hello.
End of the HTML.

Press the Enter key at the end of each line.

5 Check your code

Look through your code and compare it with the code above. Check you have typed all the code and symbols in each line correctly.

6 Save

 Click **File > Save**.

Keep saving your work regularly!

Now, your first HTML page is ready. Next, we need to find out how to view it.

AUTO-COMPLETE

You might wonder why we saved the file before we start typing any code. This was to tell the text editor we are typing HTML.

After you have made a few games you will start to remember parts of HTML. Auto-complete will help make sure your code is typed correctly.

Viewing Your Page

On pages 4–5 you learned how to create a web page. Now, we will find out how to view the page. Like all HTML pages, we will do this with a web browser.

1 Open your Documents folder

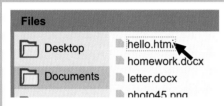

Files

📁 Desktop 📄 hello.html
📁 Documents 📄 homework.docx
  📄 letter.docx
  📄 photo45.png

Open your Documents folder and double-click the **hello.html** file.

2 View your page

🔄 **documents/hello.html**

Hello

Your web page should appear, looking like this. Congratulations!

Don't worry if it isn't working yet.

❗ Check for errors

If your page doesn't work then go back and check your code carefully.

 Make sure you typed the code exactly as shown. Check you have typed the <, > and / symbols correctly.

 Then, save your page in the text editor again, and refresh your web page.

3 Make some changes

Go back to your text editor and try changing your code.

```
1 <html>
2     <h1>Hello everybody!</h1>
3 </html>
```

Add some more text to the code. Make sure it still ends correctly.

4 Save your file

Click **File** > **Save**.

File Edit Selecti
New File
Open..
Save

5 Refresh

 Click the **Refresh** button in your web browser.

6 View the changes

🔄 **documents/hello.html**

Hello everybody!

The changes should show up in your web browser. If it doesn't work, go back and check your code very carefully.

Repeat Steps 3 to 6, practising making more small changes.

HTML & JavaScript

So far, we have made a simple web page using HTML. HTML is a language that can put things on a web page. To make the things on a web page move around, we need to use another language called JavaScript. These two languages are used together to make online and mobile games.

 Here are some of the things we'll be using JavaScript to do.

 Timers
We will use timers to repeat sections of code up to 100 times every second.

Variables
 These will keep track of things like the score in a game or the coordinates of an image.

 Random numbers
So games are different each time, we will use code to move images to random places.

 Keyboard listeners
These make code run when a particular key is pressed.

 Mouse listeners
These can make code run when something is clicked or the mouse is moved.

 Canvas
This is a special HTML object that JavaScript can draw images and shapes on.

Functions
`moveIt()` Functions are a way to reuse sections of code, and keep it organised and easy to read.

 Sound
Audio elements can load sound files. JavaScript makes these play with code.

ARRANGING YOUR SCREEN

It's useful to be able to see your code and the web browser at the same time. That way, you can make changes to your code and easily see the effect. If your screen is big enough, you should try to arrange your screen like this:

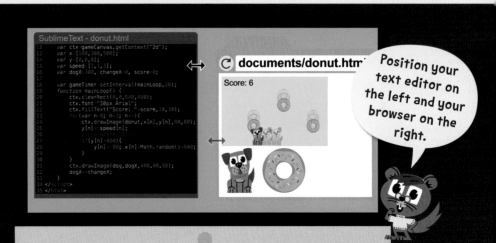

Position your text editor on the left and your browser on the right.

Pop the Balloon

Score:5

This simple game will introduce the basics of making a game using HTML and JavaScript. A balloon will move randomly around the screen while the player tries to click on it as fast as possible. A variable will keep track of the score.

You need to download a text editor to type your code – see page 4.

HOW THE GAME WORKS

Our code will use a picture of a balloon from the web.

A timer will move the balloon every 1,000 milliseconds (every second).

If the balloon gets clicked, the score will go up and the balloon will shrink down in size for a moment.

score=5

The **score** variable will keep track of how many times the balloon gets clicked and popped.

count=20

The **count** variable will count how many chances the player has had to click the balloon.

The balloon's position will be set randomly each time it moves.

moveIt()

This function will move the balloon.

clickedIt()

This function will run when it has been clicked.

1 Make a new HTML file

Open your text editor or click **File > New File**.

2 Save your file

Click **File > Save**.

Save as: pop.html ← — Type in **pop.html** as the file name.

Documents ← — Browse to your Documents folder.

Save ← Click **Save**.

3 Start coding!

Type in the first part of your code. This will include the normal start and end of the file, plus the style section.

```
1  <!doctype html> ←                                      Set the document type.
2  <html> ←                                               Start of the HTML.
3  <h1 id='scoreBox'></h1> ←                              Add a place to show the score.
4  <style> ←                                              Start of the style section.
5     #balloon{position:absolute; ←                       We will be setting the position using coordinates.
6         -webkit-transition:all 0.2s; ←                  Make any changes happen over 0.2 seconds.
7         height:160px;} ←                                The balloon will be 160 pixels high.
8  </style> ←                                             End of the style section.
9  <img id='balloon' src='https://maxw.com/b1.png'> ←    The balloon picture.
10 </html> ←                                              End of the HTML.
```

Later on you can experiment and make changes to the code, but keep it like this for now.

The transition code means changes will be animated.

4 View the page

Open your Documents folder and double-click the **pop.html** file.

C **documents/pop.html**

Your page should look like this.

If your page looks okay, go to Step 5.

! Check for errors

If your page doesn't work then go back and check your code carefully.

<> Make sure you typed the code exactly as shown. Check things like the < and > symbols are correct.

If you see this small icon instead of a balloon you have made a mistake in line 9, so check it carefully.

See pages 76–77 for more help with finding mistakes in your code.

5 Add some JavaScript

We will now start adding some JavaScript to the page. This will deal with what happens when the balloon is clicked. Move your cursor to the start of line 10 and press **Enter**. Then, add this code:

```
10 <script>                                          ← Start of the script section.
11     balloon.addEventListener('click',clickedIt);  ← Check if the balloon is clicked.
12     var score=0, count=0;                         ← Create variables to store the score
                                                         and count the balloons.
13
14     function clickedIt(){                          ← Run this code if the balloon is clicked:
15         score++;                                   ← Increase the score.
16         scoreBox.innerHTML='score:'+score;         ← Show the score.
17         balloon.style.height='1px';                ← Make the balloon shrink to 1 pixel high.
18     }                                              ← End of the clickedIt function.
19 </script>                                          ← End of the JavaScript.
20 </html>                                            ← End of the HTML.
```

6 Save

In your text editor, click **File > Save**.

HAS IT BEEN CLICKED?

To check when the mouse clicks something, we can add a **listener** to the balloon.

This code will make the function called **clickedIt** run every time the balloon is clicked.

7 Refresh

 Click the **Refresh** button in your web browser.

8 Test the code

Try clicking the balloon.

It should shrink and the score should show as 1.

If the code works, go to Step 9.

C documents/pop.html

score:1

! Check for errors

If the balloon doesn't shrink then repeat Steps 6 and 7. Check your code carefully. You may have made one of these mistakes:

Aa clickedIt scoreBox ✓
clickedit Scorebox ✗

, ; Make sure you put semicolons at the end of lines 11, 12, 15, 16 and 17.

{ } Use the correct curly brackets.

Check each line of your code very carefully to make sure it is exactly the same as the code in Step 5. Save and refresh your code again. Now, try clicking the balloon.

Still not working? See pages 76–77 to help you find where the error may be.

POSITIONING IMAGES

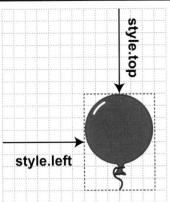

We can position an image by setting its left and top style properties.

To position an image using JavaScript we need to set its left and top style properties.

We also need to set the units we are using. Instead of using metres or centimetres we will use pixels.

```
balloon.style.left=50+'px';
balloon.style.top=100+'px';
```

This code would position the balloon 50 pixels from the left, 100 pixels down from the top.

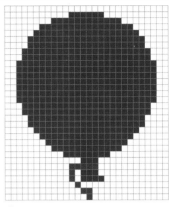

Computer screens are made up of tiny squares called **pixels**.

Help!

9   Make it move!

The final part of the code will make the balloon move. Edit lines 19 and 20 and add this code:

```
19·     function moveIt(){
20          balloon.style.height='160px';
21          balloon.style.left=Math.random()*800+'px';
22          balloon.style.top=Math.random()*600+'px';
23          count++;
24·         if(count==20){
25              alert('game over!');
26              clearInterval(timer);
27          }
28      }
29
30      var timer=setInterval(moveIt, 1000);
31 </script>
32 </html>
```

Code a function to move the balloon with this code:
Set its height.
Move the balloon to a new random position on the screen.
Increase the count.
If it has counted 20 moves then run this code:
Show a message to the player, then stop the timer running so that the game ends.
End of the function.

Make a timer that will run the **moveIt** function every 1,000 milliseconds (every second).

Lines 21 and 22 use this idea to make the balloon move to a random place.

RANDOM NUMBERS

Lots of games use random numbers. If they didn't, the game would be the same each time you played it.

`Math.random()`

This gives us a number between 0 and 1. This could be 0.5, 0.01, 0.75 or 0.99.

`Math.random()*600`

By multiplying by 600, this returns (gives us) a number between 0 and 600, such as 200, 12, 534 or 87.5.

*means **multiply** in JavaScript.

10 Save the code

In the text editor, click **File** > **Save**.

11 Refresh

 Click the **Refresh** button in your web browser.

12 Test the game

See how many times you can click the balloon as it darts around the screen!

documents/pop.html

score:5

If the game works okay, try some of the coding challenges!

Click Refresh to play the game again.

! Check for errors

If the game doesn't work then repeat Steps 10 and 11. Next, check your code — you may have made one of these mistakes:

 Check you have typed lines 20 and 21 correctly and not mixed up any symbols.

 Lines 23 and 24 need:
++ (means increase by 1).
== (means compare).

 Check you have typed all the correct brackets you need.

Look through each line of your code and make sure it is exactly the same as the code on page 13. Save and refresh your code again to see if it works.

Challenges

- Change the message at the end of the game (edit line 25).
- Can you make the game go on for longer? (Change the number in line 24.)
- Can you make the balloon move around the whole of the web page? Which numbers work best in lines 21 and 22 on your computer?
- What happens if you change the value from 1000 to 2000 in line 30?
- In line 6, try using a larger value than 0.2s – maybe 1s. Does the game get easier?

Here is the complete code for the game.

```
 1 <!doctype html>
 2 <html>
 3 <h1 id='scoreBox'></h1>
 4 <style>
 5     #balloon{position:absolute;
 6         -webkit-transition:all 0.2s;
 7         height:160px;}
 8 </style>
 9 <img id='balloon' src='https://maxw.com/b1.png'>
10 <script>
11     balloon.addEventListener('click',clickedIt);
12     var score=0, count=0;
13
14     function clickedIt(){
15         score++;
16         scoreBox.innerHTML='score:'+score;
17         balloon.style.height='1px';
18     }
19     function moveIt(){
20         balloon.style.height='160px';
21         balloon.style.left=Math.random()*800+'px';
22         balloon.style.top=Math.random()*600+'px';
23         count++;
24         if(count==20){
25             alert('game over!');
26             clearInterval(timer);
27         }
28     }
29
30     var timer=setInterval(moveIt, 1000);
31 </script>
32 </html>
```

JavaScript Tennis

In this project you will learn how to make a simple tennis game. The ball will bounce around the screen while the player controls a bat using the mouse. The bat and ball will both be special HTML elements called divs. Divs can have their colour and shape set with code.

HOW THE GAME WORKS

Code will be used to set the colour and size of the bat and ball. By setting a special **border-radius** property we will make the ball round.

x,y — The **x** and **y** variables will store where the ball is.

batX — This variable will store the x position of the bat.

 The bat will move left or right to match the x position of the mouse.

A timer will move the ball 100 times every second.

 speedX *speedY* — These two variables will store how fast the ball is moving sideways (**speedX**) and up or down (**speedY**).

 If the ball hits the side, we will make it bounce by changing the **speedX** variable.

 If it hits the top, we will change the **speedY** variable.

moveBat() — This function will move the bat.

moveBall() — This function will move the ball.

14

① Make a new HTML file

Open your text editor or click **File > New File**.

② Save your file

Click **File > Save**.

Save as: tennis.html ← Type in **tennis.html** as the file name.

Documents ← Browse to your Documents folder.

Save Click **Save**.

③ Start coding!

Type in the first part of your code. This will include the normal start and end of the file, plus a style section that we will use to set the colours and sizes of elements used in the game.

```
1  <!doctype html> ←                                    Set the document type.
2  <html> ←                                             Start of the HTML.
3  <style> ←                                            Start of the style section.
4      #board{position:absolute; ←                      Set the style for the
5          width:550px; height:450px;                   board div.
6          background-color:lightgreen;}
7      #bat{position:absolute;          ←               Set the style for
8          top:420px; width:80px; height:20px;          the bat div.
9          background-color:blue;}
10     #ball{position:absolute; ←                        Set the style for
11         width:48px; height:48px;                      the ball div.
12         border-radius:24px;
13         background-color:yellow;}
14 </style> ←                                            End of the style section.
15 </html> ←                                             End of the HTML.
```

> The border-radius property turns the ball div into a circle.

You can make changes to the size and colour of the bat, ball and board later on, but keep them like this for now.

④ View the page

Open your Documents folder and double-click the **tennis.html** file.

> The page will be blank but we will open it now so it is ready for the next steps.

documents/tennis.html

 Move left!

⑤ Add the divs

Now, we need to add the div elements to the page. These divs will become the game board, ball and bat. Edit line 15 and add this code:

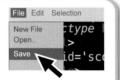

```
15  <body onmousemove="moveBat(event)">
16      <div id='board'></div>
17      <div id='bat'></div>
18      <div id='ball'></div>
19  </body>
20  </html>
```

*Start the main body of the HTML page. Add a **listener** to check when the mouse moves.*

← *Add the **board** div.*
← *Add the **bat** div.*
← *Add the **ball** div.*
← *End of the body section.*
← *End of the HTML.*

To detect when the mouse moves, we will use a **listener**.

This code will make a function called **moveBat** run every time the mouse is moved.

The function will be able to tell exactly where the mouse pointer is.

⑥ Save

In your text editor, click **File > Save**.

File Edit Selection
New File
Open..
Save

If your code still doesn't work, see page 76–77 to get more help.

⑦ Refresh the browser

Click the **Refresh** button.

Your page should look like this. If it does then go to Step 8.

⟳ **documents/tennis.html**

⚠ Check for errors

If it looks wrong then you may have made one of these mistakes. Check your code!

Wrong shape board — check line 4.

Missing ball — check lines 10–13 and line 18.

Missing bat — check lines 7–9 and line 17.

Line 22 should be empty. Coders leave some lines blank to make it easier to read their code.

event.clientX gives the x value of the mouse pointer coordinates.

⑧ Get moving

Edit line 20 and add this next section of code to get the bat moving:

```
20  <script>
21      var x=100,y=100,speedX=2,speedY=2,batX=0;
22
23      function moveBat(event){
24          batX=event.clientX;
25          bat.style.left=batX+'px';
26      }
27  </script>
28  </html>
```

← *Start of the JavaScript.*
← *Declare all the variables we need.*

When the bat moves, run this code:
*Set **batX** to be the same as the x position of the mouse.*
Position the bat.
End of the function.
End of the script.

See pages 76–77 to help you find where the error may be.

9 Save the code

Click **File** > **Save**.

10 Refresh

 Click the **Refresh** button in your web browser.

11 Test your work

Try moving your mouse left and right. The bat should move across the screen.

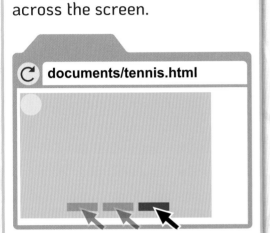

documents/tennis.html

If it works okay, go to Step 12.

! Check for errors

If the blue bat doesn't move then repeat Steps 9 and 10. You may have made one of the mistakes below, so check your code:

Aa moveBat batX clientX ✓
movebat batx clientx ✗

, ; Check line 21 carefully. Make sure you put semicolons at the end of lines 24 and 25.

{ } Use the correct curly brackets.

12 Move and bounce

This final part of the code will get the ball moving. Edit line 27 and add this code:

```
27      function moveBall(){
28          x=x+speedX;
29          y=y+speedY;
30          ball.style.left=x+'px';
31          ball.style.top=y+'px';
32
33          if(x>530)speedX=-2;
34          if(x<0)speedX=2;
35          if(y<0)speedY=2;
36          if((y>372)&&(Math.abs(batX-x)<60)){speedY=-2;}
37          if(y>450){
38              alert('game over!');
39              clearInterval(timer);
40          }
41      }
42
43      var timer=setInterval(moveBall, 10);
44 </script>
45 </html>
```

Code a function that moves the ball with this code:

Change the x and y variables by the speedX and speedY variables.

Set the ball's position using the x and y variables.

If the ball reaches the right edge, left edge or top of the screen, make it bounce.

If the ball hits the bat then make it bounce.

If the ball goes below the bat and reaches the bottom of the screen, show a message and stop the timer running.

End of the function.

Start a timer that will run the moveBall function every 10 milliseconds.

Click **File** > **Save**.

 Click the **Refresh** button in your web browser.

See page 76–77 to help you find where the error may be.

Test your work

The ball should bounce around the screen. Try to keep it bouncing with your bat.

C documents/tennis.html

 *Why not try the challenges if everything works?*

 Check for errors

If the code doesn't work, do Steps 13 and 14 again. Check your code in case you made one of these mistakes:

Aa
| speedX | speedY | moveBall ✓ |
| speedx | speedy | moveball ✗ |

' ; Make sure you have typed all the semicolons. Line 36 is tricky, so check it carefully.

 If the ball doesn't bounce properly, check you haven't mixed up +2 and -2, and that the other values are correct.

Click Refresh to play the game again.

Challenges

- Try changing the colours of the board, bat and ball. See page 77 for more information on all the colours you can use.

- Find out what happens if you change the **border-radius** value from 24px to a smaller number.

- Can you make the ball move more quickly?

- If you have a large screen you could make the game board larger in the style section. You will also need to alter the code that checks when the ball should bounce.

- Add a score variable to the game. Make it increase whenever the ball bounces. You could show the score at the end of the game by changing line 38.

Here is the complete code for the game.

```html
1  <!doctype html>
2  <html>
3  <style>
4      #board{position:absolute;
5          width:550px; height:450px;
6          background-color:lightgreen;}
7      #bat{position:absolute;
8          top:420px; width:80px; height:20px;
9          background-color:blue;}
10     #ball{position:absolute;
11         width:48px; height:48px;
12         border-radius:24px;
13         background-color:yellow;}
14 </style>
15 <body onmousemove="moveBat(event)">
16     <div id='board'></div>
17     <div id='bat'></div>
18     <div id='ball'></div>
19 </body>
20 <script>
21     var x=100,y=100,speedX=2,speedY=2,batX=0;
22
23     function moveBat(event){
24         batX=event.clientX;
25         bat.style.left=batX+'px';
26     }
27     function moveBall(){
28         x=x+speedX;
29         y=y+speedY;
30         ball.style.left=x+'px';
31         ball.style.top=y+'px';
32
33         if(x>530)speedX=-2;
34         if(x<0)speedX=2;
35         if(y<0)speedY=2;
36         if((y>372)&&(Math.abs(batX-x)<60)){speedY=-2;}
37         if(y>450){
38             alert('game over!');
39             clearInterval(timer);
40         }
41     }
42
43     var timer=setInterval(moveBall, 10);
44 </script>
45 </html>
```

Catch It!

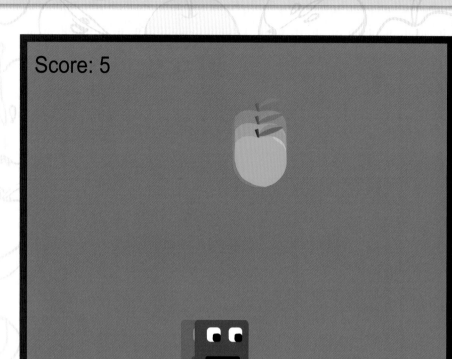

Score: 5

This project will introduce you to another way of creating games using JavaScript. A special HTML element called the canvas will be used. The canvas gives us a place to draw objects in a game. In this game, a monster controlled by the player has to catch as many falling apples as possible.

HOW THE GAME WORKS

Pictures of an apple and a monster will be loaded from the web.

score=3 The **score** variable will count how many apples get eaten.

x,y These store the apple's coordinates.

monsterX
changeX These hold the **x** value of the monster, and how much it should move.

Copies of the monster and the apple will be drawn onto the canvas using the **drawImage** command.

 A timer will run the **mainLoop** function every 20 milliseconds. It will move the apples down and show the score so far.

 A second timer will stop the game after 30 seconds.

checkForHits() This function will check if the monster is near enough to the apple to eat it.

gameOver() This will stop the game.

 If the apple gets to the bottom of the screen or gets eaten, it will move to a new random position at the top.

  The **Left** and **Right** arrow keys will set **changeX** to be 2 or -2 (minus 2). This makes the monster move left or right.

1 Make a new HTML file

Open your text editor or click **File > New File**.

2 Save your file

Click **File > Save**.

Save as: catch.html

Documents

Type in **catch.html** as the file name.

Browse to your Documents folder.

Save Click **Save**.

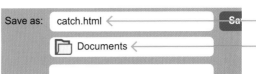

3 Start coding!

Type in the first part of your code. This will include the normal start and end of the file, plus a place for the script to be added.

```
1  <!doctype html>
2  <html>
3  <div style='background-color:dodgerblue; width:640px;'>
4      <canvas id="gameCanvas" width="640" height="480"></canvas>
5  </div>
6  <div style='display:block;'>
7      <img id='apple' src='https://maxw.com/apple.png'>
8      <img id='monster' src='https://maxw.com/monster3.png'>
9  </div>
10 <script>
11 </script>
12 </html>
```

This div sets the background colour for the game.

Add the game canvas.

This div holds the images.

The images we will load for the game.

The JavaScript will be added here.

SINGLE OR DOUBLE QUOTES?

You can use single quotes or double quotes in your code but you need to make sure they match.

`id='apple'` ✓ `id="apple"` ✓
`id="apple'` ✗ `id='apple"` ✗

4 View the page

Open your Documents folder and double-click the **catch.html** file.

 Your page should look like this.

⟳ **documents/catch.html**

If your page looks okay, go to Step 5.

We are just loading the pictures here. Later on, we will draw them on the canvas.

! Check for errors

If your page doesn't look right then check all your code.

<> Make sure you typed the code exactly as shown. All the symbols need to be typed correctly.

If you see this small icon instead of the apple, check line 7. If you can't see the monster, check line 8.

5 Drop the apple

Now for the JavaScript code. We will start by making some variables, and then add code to get the apple moving down the screen.

```
11      var ctx=gameCanvas.getContext("2d");
12      var x=300, y=50, monsterX=300, changeX=0, score=0;
13
14      var gameTimer=setInterval(mainLoop,20);
15      function mainLoop() {
16          ctx.clearRect(0,0,640,480);
17          ctx.font="30px Arial";
18          ctx.fillText("Score: "+score,10,30);
19          ctx.drawImage(apple,x,y,80,80);
20          y+=3;
21          if(y>480){y=-80; x=Math.random()*600;}
22          ctx.drawImage(monster,monsterX,400,80,80);
23          monsterX+=changeX;
24          //checkForHits();
25      }
26  </script>
27  </html>
```

By using a variable to point to the canvas it makes it much simpler for us to use it.

Get all the other variables ready.

This runs the mainLoop function.
The function runs the code below:
Clear the whole canvas.
Choose the font size.
Show the score in the corner.
Draw the apple.
Move the apple down.
Has the apple hit the bottom?
Draw the monster.
Move the monster left or right (we will add code later to make this line work).

Check for catches. The two slashes stop the game trying to run the function yet.

We can't run the checkForHit function yet as we haven't coded it!

6 Save

In your text editor, click **File > Save**.

7 Refresh

 Click the **Refresh** button in your web browser.

8 Test your work

The apple should fall down the screen. When it gets to the bottom it should start again from the top.

(The monster won't move yet and the score won't change.)

C documents/catch.html

Score: 0

! Check for errors

If the code doesn't work, do Steps 6 and 7 again. Then, check your code in case you made one of these mistakes:

 If there is no small apple then check line 19.

 If the apple doesn't move, check lines 14 and 20. If it only falls once, check line 21.

 No small monster? Have a look at line 22.

See page 76-77 to help you find where the error may be.

THE CANVAS

The canvas is a special HTML element that can be added to a web page. It is very useful in game coding. It can be used to draw lines or shapes in millions of different colours. Images can be drawn onto the canvas at particular coordinates. By clearing the canvas then changing an object's coordinates, we can create animation in a game.

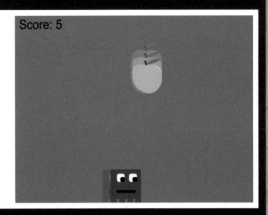

Score: 5

Adding the canvas

```
<canvas id="gameCanvas" width="640" height="480"></canvas>
```

Firstly, the canvas must be added to the HTML page using this code. The width and height are set in pixels.

Using the canvas

```
var ctx=gameCanvas.getContext("2d");
```

We need a way to "address" the part of the canvas that can show graphics. This means we need a way to send it commands. Most coders do this by making a variable called **ctx** — which is short for context.

Adding text

```
ctx.fillText("Score: "+score,10,30);
```

We can add text anywhere on the canvas by using this command. The **ctx.font** command can be used to set the font and font size.

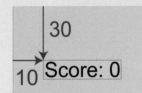

This code writes the score on the canvas at the coordinates (10,30).

Erasing part of the canvas

```
ctx.clearRect(0,0,320,240);
```

To create animation we need to keep moving things and updating the canvas. Before we draw an image in a new place, we usually need to erase everything. The **clearRect** command does this.

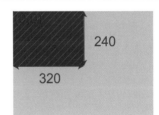

This code clears a 320 x 240 rectangle on the canvas, starting at the coordinates (0,0).

Adding an image

```
ctx.drawImage(apple,60,30,80,80);
```

This command draws an **<img>** element onto the canvas. The image element must be loaded in the HTML section of the document.

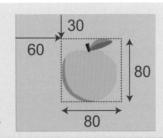

*This code draws an 80 x 80 copy of the image called **apple** onto the canvas at the coordinates (60,30).*

9 Left and right keys

The monster needs to move left or right when the arrow keys are pressed. We will add a **listener** to our code to do this.

We need to know when the Left or Right arrow keys are pressed.

```
26      document.onkeydown=keyPressed;
27      function keyPressed(e){
28          var k=e.keyCode;
29          if(k==37){changeX=-2;}
30          if(k==39){changeX=2;}
31      }
32  </script>
33  </html>
```

*Add a listener that calls a function named **keyPressed**.*

*This function will store a code in the **k** variable, showing which key was pressed.*

*If **k** equals 37 then the **Left** arrow key was pressed, so set **changeX** to **-2**.*
*If **k** is 39 then it was the **Right** arrow key, so set **changeX** to **2**.*

WHICH KEY WAS PRESSED?

In the previous games, we have used **listeners** to check when the mouse is moved or clicked. The **onkeydown** listener will "call" the **keyPressed** function when a key is pressed down.

Different keys will give different code values.

Key	Code		Key	Code		Key	Code
A	65		L	76		W	87
B	66		M	77		X	88
C	67		N	78		Y	89
D	68		O	79		Z	90
E	69		P	80		SPACE	32
F	70		Q	81		ENTER	13
G	71		R	82		SHIFT	16
H	72		S	83		←	37
I	73		T	84		→	39
J	74		U	85		↑	38
K	75		V	86		↓	40

10 Save & Refresh

In your text editor, click **File** > **Save**.

 Click the **Refresh** button in your web browser.

11 Test your work

Click the middle of the game so that any key presses are sent to it. Try using the arrow keys to move the monster left and right.

 **documents/catch.html**

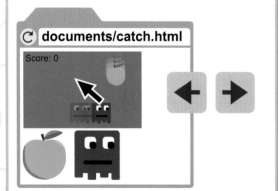

! Check for errors

Problems with your code? Start by saving your code and refreshing the page. Check all your code carefully.

 If the monster moves in the wrong direction when the keys are pressed, check you haven't mixed up parts of lines 29 and 30.

For some tips to set focus, see mod A on page 72.

GETTING FOCUS

A program needs to know it is being used for key presses to work. For example, your text editor only lets you type in it if you click it first. This is called **having focus**.

Before testing a game that uses keyboard listeners, you need to click the game first. This means it will have focus. Remember to click the game before testing it works okay.

12 Has the apple been caught?

To see if the monster has caught the apple, we will make a function.
It will work out how close together they are.

```
32      function checkForHits(){          Define the function.
33          if((Math.abs(400-y)<60)&&      Test if they are less than 60 pixels apart vertically...
34          (Math.abs(monsterX-x)<60)){     ...and if they are less than 60 pixels apart horizontally.
35              score+=1;                   Increase the score by 1.
36              y=-80; x=Math.random()*600;  Move the apple to a random position near the top.
37          }                               End of the if code.
38      }
39 </script>
40 </html>
```

```
24          checkForHits();
```

Go back to line 24 and delete the two slashes that were there until the function was ready.

13 Save & Refresh

In your text editor, click **File > Save**.

 Refresh the web browser.

14 Test your work

When the monster catches an apple, the score should go up. The apple should jump to a new position and start falling.

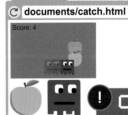
documents/catch.html
Score: 4

Check for errors

Problems? Save, refresh and check your code. Have you mixed up any of the symbols?

Mind out!

Yum!

15 Game Over!

We will add a timer that calls (runs) a function after 30 seconds.
The function will show a message and stop the game.

```
39        setTimeout(gameOver,30000);        ← Make a timer to call the gameOver function
40        function gameOver(){               ←   after 30,000 milliseconds (30 seconds).
41            clearInterval(gameTimer);      ← Define the function.
42            ctx.font="80px Arial";         ← Stop the timer that runs the mainLoop function.
43            ctx.fillText("Game Over!",100,250) ← Set the font style.
44        }                                  ← Show a message.
45 </script>
46 </html>
```

```
6 <div style='display:none;'>
```

Now that the images have been loaded, we can hide them. Change the style in line 6 to **display:none**.

16 Save & Refresh

Click **File > Save** then **Refresh** the browser.

17 Test your game

The game should now be fully working. What can you score before 30 seconds are up?

documents/catch.html

Score: 9

Game Over!

! Check for errors

Problems? Check the last few lines of your code carefully, then click **Save** and **Refresh**.

Aa

gameOver fillText gameTimer ✓
GameOver fillText Gametimer ✗

( )

Make sure you have added all the brackets correctly.

Click Refresh to play the game again.

Mmm!

Challenges

- Delete **dodgerblue** in line 3 and type in another colour. What happens? See page 77 for a list of colour names that will work.

- Make the apple move more quickly by editing line 20. Can you make the monster move faster? You'll need to change part of lines 29 and 30.

- Change the code so that each apple is worth 5 points.

- Make the game work with different keys on the keyboard. Use the table on page 24 to help.

- Make the game run for 1 minute instead of 30 seconds.

```
1  <!doctype html>
2  <html>
3  <div style='background-color:dodgerblue; width:640px;'>
4      <canvas id="gameCanvas" width="640" height="480"></canvas>
5  </div>
6  <div style='display:none;'>
7      <img id='apple' src='https://maxw.com/apple.png'>
8      <img id='monster' src='https://maxw.com/monster3.png'>
9  </div>
10 <script>
11     var ctx=gameCanvas.getContext("2d");
12     var x=300, y=50, monsterX=300, changeX=0, score=0;
13
14     var gameTimer=setInterval(mainLoop,20);
15     function mainLoop() {
16         ctx.clearRect(0,0,640,480);
17         ctx.font="30px Arial";
18         ctx.fillText("Score: "+score,10,30);
19         ctx.drawImage(apple,x,y,80,80);
20         y+=3;
21         if(y>480){y=-80; x=Math.random()*600;}
22         ctx.drawImage(monster,monsterX,400,80,80);
23         monsterX+=changeX;
24         checkForHits();
25     }
26     document.onkeydown=keyPressed;
27     function keyPressed(e){
28         var k=e.keyCode;
29         if(k==37){changeX=-2;}
30         if(k==39){changeX=2;}
31     }
32     function checkForHits(){
33         if((Math.abs(400-y)<60)&&
34             (Math.abs(monsterX-x)<60)){
35             score+=1;
36             y=-80; x=Math.random()*600;
37         }
38     }
39     setTimeout(gameOver,30000);
40     function gameOver(){
41         clearInterval(gameTimer);
42         ctx.font="80px Arial";
43         ctx.fillText("Game Over!",100,250);
44     }
45 </script>
46 </html>
```

Here is the complete code for the game.

Dog 'n' Donuts

You should code Catch It! before coding this game.

Score: 17

Dog 'n' Donuts uses similar techniques to the previous catching game. But instead of one object falling down the screen, there are three. To code this we will use something called an array. This is a special sort of variable that can store multiple values. We will also add a simple sound effect to the game.

HOW THE GAME WORKS

 Pictures of a donut and Smuffy the dog will be loaded from a website.

score=8 This variable will count how many donuts get eaten.

dogX=30 This will store the x position of the dog.

x=[ ]
y=[ ]
speed=[ ]

The position and speed of the donuts will be kept in **arrays**. These are a bit like lists.

 A sound effect will play when a donut is caught. It will be loaded from a website.

 A timer will run the **mainLoop** function every 20 milliseconds. It will move the donuts down and show the score so far.

checkForHits() This function will check how far away a particular donut is from the dog.

gameOver() This will stop the game.

 Each donut will move to a new random position at the top after it reaches the bottom or gets eaten.

  The **Left** and **Right** arrow keys will set **changeX** to be 4 or -4. This will move the dog left or right. The **keyPressed** function will make this work.

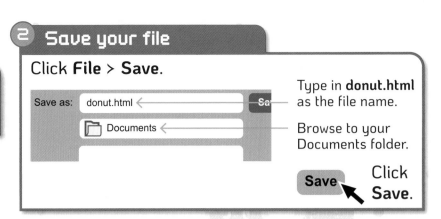

File | Edit
New File

Open your text editor or click **File > New File**.

② **Save your file**

Click **File > Save**.

Save as: donut.html

📁 Documents

Type in **donut.html** as the file name.

Browse to your Documents folder.

Save Click **Save**.

③ **Start coding!**

You will recognise some of this code from the previous game. Type it in carefully.

```
1  <!doctype html>
2  <html>
3  <audio id='beep' src='https://maxw.com/beep2.mp3'></audio>
4  <div style='background-color:gold; width:640px;'>
5      <canvas id="gameCanvas" width="640" height="480"></canvas>
6  </div>
7  <div style='display:block;'>
8      <img id='dog' src='https://maxw.com/smuffy.png'>
9      <img id='donut' src='https://maxw.com/donut.png'>
10 </div>
11 <script>
12 </script>
13 </html>
```

— Load in a sound file.

This acts as a background.

← The game canvas.

The images are held here.

— The images we will load for the game.

— The JavaScript will be added here.

SINGLE OR DOUBLE QUOTES?

You can use single quotes or double quotes in your code but you need to make sure they match.

id='apple' ✓   id="apple" ✓
id="apple' ✗   id='apple" ✗

④ **View the page**

Double-click the **donut.html** file.

↻ **documents/donut.html**

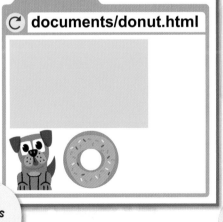

If your page looks like this, go on to Step 5.

❗ **Check for errors**

Check all your code if the page looks wrong.

 All the symbols need to be typed correctly. Make sure you typed the code exactly as shown.

 If you see this icon instead of the dog, check line 8. If your donut is missing then check line 9.

I'm so hungry!

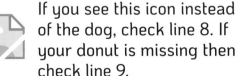

5   Drop the donuts

Now for the JavaScript code. We will start by making some variables, and then add code to get the apple moving down the screen.

```
12        var ctx=gameCanvas.getContext("2d");
13        var x=[100,300,500];
14        var y=[0,0,0];
15        var speed=[2,1,3];
16        var dogX=300, changeX=0, score=0;
17
18        var gameTimer=setInterval(mainLoop,20);
19        function mainLoop() {
20            ctx.clearRect(0,0,640,480);
21            ctx.font="30px Arial";
22            ctx.fillText("Score: "+score,10,30);
23            for(var n=0; n<3; n++){
24                ctx.drawImage(donut,x[n],y[n],80,80);
25                y[n]+=speed[n];
26                //checkForHits(n);
27                if(y[n]>480){
28                    y[n]=-80; x[n]=Math.random()*600;
29                }
30            }
31            ctx.drawImage(dog,dogX,400,80,80);
32            dogX+=changeX;
33        }
34 </script>
35 </html>
```

*The **ctx** variable will be used when we want to code the canvas.*

Create three arrays to store the x, y and speed values of each of the falling donuts.

Get the other variables ready.

Clear the whole canvas.
Choose the font size.
Show the score in the corner.
Run the code below for each donut:
Position the donut at its x & y values.
Move it down by its speed value.
Has it been caught yet? The slashes stop the function running for now.
If it has reached the bottom of the screen then move it back to the top.
End of the donut loop.
Draw the dog.
Move the dog left or right.

6   Save

In your text editor, click **File > Save**.

7   Refresh

Click the **Refresh** button in your web browser.

ARRAYS

Arrays are a great way to add multiple images to a game. You can write the code for one donut, and reuse the code to control 2, 3 or even 20 donuts!

```
var x=[170,400,590];
var y=[110,250,360];
```

These arrays store the values for the x and y coordinates of three donuts.

JavaScript starts counting at zero, so the first donut is called **donut0**. We can get its x value by typing x[0] in our code, and its y value from y[0]. x[1] and y[1] store **donut1**'s coordinates. x[2] and y[2] have **donut2**'s coordinates.

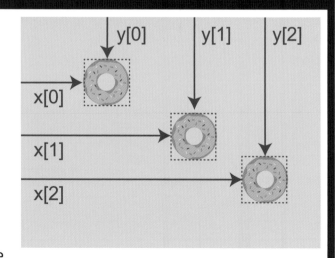

Three donuts should appear and fall down the screen. When they get to the bottom they should jump to the top and start again.

(The dog won't move yet and the score won't change.)

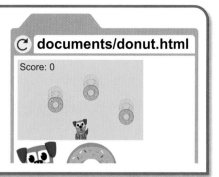

documents/donut.html

Score: 0

Let's learn some new ways to locate bugs in your code.

WHERE IS THE BUG?

There is an extra tool coders use to track down bugs — the Developer Console. This shows lots of complex things about how a website is working.

I need to find where the error in my code is!

It will also tell you the line number where the error is — really useful info!

B1. Look in the top-right corner of the browser. Click the button with three lines or three dots on it.

B2. Click **More Tools** > **Developer Tools**.

B3. The Developer Console will appear on the right.

B4. Refresh your web page.

Make sure the Console tab is selected.

B5. Any errors will be listed in the Console.

| | | Elements | **Console** | Sources | » | ⊗ 1 | | ⚙ | ⋮ | ✕ |

▶ ≔ 1 message

⊗ GET https://maxw.com/smffy.png 404 donuts.html:8

❽ No user me…

▶ ⊗ 1 error

Here is the information you need!

You may have to click the Error tab.

404   **donuts.html:8**

The type of error or error code.

The line number with the error.

B6. Now, go back to the code and look for an error in the line indicated.

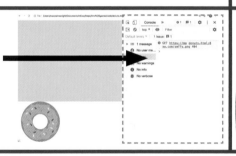

```
7   <div sty
8      <img
9      <img
```

In this case, the error was in line 8…

```
om/smuffy.png'>
com/donut.png'
```

…the file name had been typed incorrectly.

Yum!

9 Move the dog

The dog needs to move left or right when the arrow keys are pressed. Just as in the previous game, we will add a **listener** to our code to do this.

```
34      document.onkeydown=keyPressed;
35      function keyPressed(e){
36          var k=e.keyCode;
37          if(k==37){changeX=-4;}
38          if(k==39){changeX=4;}
39      }
40  </script>
41  </html>
```

*Add a listener that calls a function named **keyPressed**.*

*This function will store a code in the **k** variable, showing which key was pressed.*

*If **k** equals 37 then the **Left** arrow key was pressed, so set **changeX** to **-4**.*

*If **k** equals 39 then it was the **Right** arrow key, so set **changeX** to **4**.*

10 Save & Refresh

Click **File** > **Save** then **Refresh** the browser.

11 Test your game

Click the middle of the game so that it **has focus**. Use the arrow keys to move the dog left and right.

documents/donut.html
Score: 0

(It won't eat the donuts yet.)

! Check for errors

If the dog moves the wrong way then check you haven't mixed up some of lines 37 and 38.

Use the Developer Console to find bugs.

See page 31 for help using the Developer Console.

THE Nth DONUT

If we just typed x[0], x[1] and x[2] to check up on each donut we'd end up writing quite a lot of code, especially if we added more donuts.

```
var x=[170,400,590];
var y=[110,250,360];
```

Instead, we can make a variable called **n** and start it off with **n** set to 0. We can then type **x[n]** in our code. To find the next **x** value in the list, we just need to change **n** from 0 to 1.

This idea is used to make the **checkForHits** function work – and in almost all games coded with JavaScript.

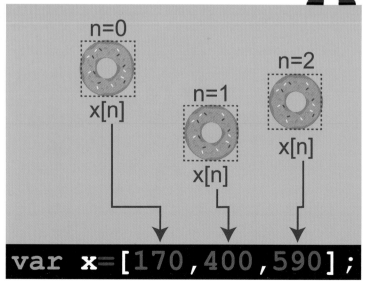

n=0
x[n]

n=1
x[n]

n=2
x[n]

```
var x=[170,400,590];
```

12 Has the dog caught a donut?

To check if the dog has eaten a donut, we will make a function. We will need to tell the function which of the three donuts to check. To do this, we will send it a number — this is called **passing a parameter**.

```
40    function checkForHits(n){          ← Define the function.
41        if((Math.abs(400-y[n])<60)&&    ← If they are less than 60 pixels apart vertically...
42            (Math.abs(dogX-x[n])<60)){   ← ...and less than 60 pixels horizontally, then:
43            score+=1;                     ← Change the score by 1.
44            y[n]=-80; x[n]=Math.random()*600;  ← Move the donut to somewhere near the top.
45            beep.play();                  ← Play the sound effect.
46        }                                 ← End of the if code.
47    }
48 </script>
49 </html>
```

```
26                    checkForHits(n);
```
Go back to line 26 and delete the two slashes that were there until the function was ready.

13 Save & Refresh

Click **File > Save** then **Refresh** the browser.

14 Test the code

If the dog catches a donut, the score should go up and you should hear a beep. The donut should move back to the top.

C documents/donut.html

Score: 6

PLAYING SOUNDS

MP3 sound files can be played with JavaScript code. A sound file needs to be added into the HTML part of the document. This is done with an audio element:

```
<audio id='beep' src='beep2.mp3'></audio>
```

Playing a sound file is quite simple:

```
beep.play();
```

If you need to play the sound quite often, it will work better if you rewind the sound before playing it:

```
beep.currentTime=0;
```

If you want to use other sound files, make sure you download them and move them to your Documents folder.

! Check for errors

If it's not working, check you have typed all the symbols correctly — see page 77 for more help.

Sometimes, sound files will get blocked by your web browser. If you have problems coding with sounds, see page 51.

15 Game Over!

Finally, we will add a timer that calls a function after 1 minute.
The function will stop the game and show a message.

```
48      setTimeout(gameOver,60000);
49      function gameOver(){
50          clearInterval(gameTimer);
51          ctx.font="80px Arial";
52          ctx.fillText("Game Over!",100,250);
53      }
54 </script>
55 </html>
```

Make a timer to call the **gameOver** function after 60,000 milliseconds (1 minute).
Define the function.
Stop the timer that runs the **mainLoop** function.
Set the font style.
Show a "Game Over!" message.

We can hide the images we used to load the graphics. Change the style in line 7 to **display:none**.

`7 <div style='display:none;'>`

16 Save & Refresh

Click **File** > **Save** then **Refresh** the browser.

17 Test your game

The game should now be fully working. How much can you score before 1 minute is up?

documents/donut.html

Score: 15

Game Over!

! Check for errors

Not working? Check your code carefully, then **Save** and **Refresh**.

Aa gameTimer gameOver ✓
        Gametimer gameover ✗

If it's still not running, check pages 76–77 for more tips.

Click Refresh to play the game again.

Challenges

- Show a different message at the end of the game.
- Change the speed the donuts fall at and how fast the dog moves around.
- Experiment with different key combinations to find a layout you like best.
- Can you make the game work with 5 donuts? (You will need to add some more values to the arrays in lines 13, 14 and 15, and change a number in line 23.)
- See if you can find some other sound effects on your computer and use them instead.

```
 1 <!doctype html>
 2 <html>
 3 <audio id='beep' src='https://maxw.com/beep2.mp3'></audio>
 4 <div style='background-color:gold; width:640px;'>
 5     <canvas id="gameCanvas" width="640" height="480"></canvas>
 6 </div>
 7 <div style='display:none;'>
 8     <img id='dog' src='https://maxw.com/smuffy.png'>
 9     <img id='donut' src='https://maxw.com/donut.png'>
10 </div>
11 <script>
12     var ctx=gameCanvas.getContext("2d");
13     var x=[100,300,500];
14     var y=[0,0,0];
15     var speed=[2,1,3];
16     var dogX=300, changeX=0, score=0;
17
18     var gameTimer=setInterval(mainLoop,20);
19     function mainLoop() {
20         ctx.clearRect(0,0,640,480);
21         ctx.font="30px Arial";
22         ctx.fillText("Score: "+score,10,30);
23         for(var n=0; n<3; n++){
24             ctx.drawImage(donut,x[n],y[n],80,80);
25             y[n]+=speed[n];
26             checkForHits(n);
27             if(y[n]>480){
28                 y[n]=-80; x[n]=Math.random()*600;
29             }
30         }
31         ctx.drawImage(dog,dogX,400,80,80);
32         dogX+=changeX;
33     }
34     document.onkeydown=keyPressed;
35     function keyPressed(e){
36         var k=e.keyCode;
37         if(k==37){changeX=-4;}
38         if(k==39){changeX=4;}
39     }
40     function checkForHits(n){
41         if((Math.abs(400-y[n])<60)&&
42            (Math.abs(dogX-x[n])<60)){
43             score+=1;
44             y[n]=-80; x[n]=Math.random()*600;
45             beep.play();
46         }
47     }
48     setTimeout(gameOver,60000);
49     function gameOver(){
50         clearInterval(gameTimer);
51         ctx.font="80px Arial";
52         ctx.fillText("Game Over!",100,250);
53     }
54 </script>
55 </html>
```

Here is the complete code for the game.

Dogs can't eat donuts!

Flying Fish

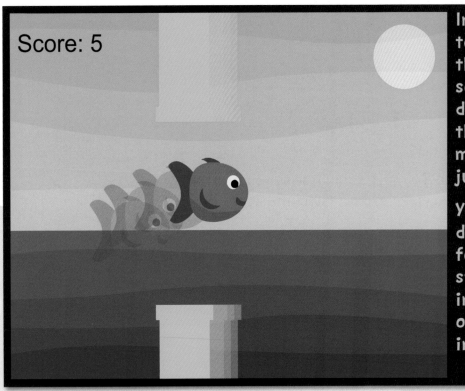

Score: 5

In this game, a fish has to jump over pipes as they scroll across the screen. We will use some different ways to move the fish up and down, making it look like it is jumping.

You will need to download the graphics for the game before starting coding. This will introduce you to ways of using the different images that you choose.

HOW THE GAME WORKS

 All images are downloaded into your Documents folder.

The sea picture will be set as a background for a div. The div will hold the game canvas. The fish and pipes will be drawn onto the canvas.

fishY  The y value of the fish will be stored in this variable.

score=5 This variable will count the score.

ySpeed This will store how fast the fish is moving up or down.

x,y These variables will store the coordinates of the pipe.

 A timer will run the **mainLoop** function every 10 milliseconds.

checkHitPipe() This will test if the fish has hit the pipe by comparing coordinates.

mainLoop() This will move the fish and pipe.

 The pipe will be positioned at the right-hand side of the screen, at a random y value. When it gets to the left-hand side, it will jump back to the right.

 Pressing any key will be picked up by the keyboard listener. It will set **ySpeed** to -2, making the fish jump up.

① Find the images

Start by finding the images you need for this game from **maxw.com/graphics**

You might try changing some of these later, but for now use these images to make sure the code works okay.

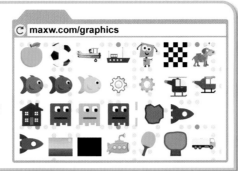

② Download a fish

Right-click the fish.

Choose **Save Image As...**

Browse to your Documents folder.

Click **Save**.

This needs to be the same folder you use to save the HTML game files in this book.

③ Download sea and pipes

Repeat Step 2 to download the green pipes and the blue sea.

④ New file

Open your text editor and start a new file.

⑤ Save

Save the code as **fish.html** in the same folder that you put the images.

⑥ Start your code

Type in the first part of your code. Include a style section.

```
1  <!doctype html>
2  <html>
3  <style>                                          Start of the style section.
4      div{width:640px; height:480px;               Any div elements will be 640 x 480 pixels in size
5          background:url('sea.png');}              and have a sea image as the background.
6      img{display:block;}                          All images will be shown (but hidden later).
7  </style>                                         End of the style section.
8  <div>                                                            The usual
9      <canvas id="gameCanvas" width="640" height="480"></canvas>  canvas for
10 </div>                                                           the game.
11 <img id='fish' src='fish.png'>                   The fish image we downloaded.
12 <img id='pipes' src='pipes.png'>                 The downloaded pipes image.
13 </html>
```

7 View the page

Double-click the **fish.html** file.

↻ **documents/fish.html**

You may have to scroll down to see the green pipes.

! Check for errors

If you see this icon instead of one of the three pictures then check you have downloaded them to the correct folder.

Still having problems? Use the Developer Console – see page 31 for help using it.

8 Add some JavaScript

We will start by coding the **mainLoop** function for the game. It will move the pipes across the screen and draw the fish and score on the canvas.

```
13  <script>
14      var ctx=gameCanvas.getContext("2d");
15      var x=640, y=-160, fishY=220, ySpeed=0, score=0;
16
17      function mainLoop() {
18          ctx.clearRect(0, 0, 640, 480);
19          ctx.drawImage(pipes,x,y,80,800);
20          x+=-2;
21          //checkHitPipe();
22          if(x<-80){
23              x=640; y=Math.random()*-320;
24              score++;
25          }
26          ctx.drawImage(fish,10,fishY,80,80);
27          ctx.font="30px Arial";
28          ctx.fillText("Score: "+score, 10, 30);
29          ySpeed+=0.02;
30          fishY+=ySpeed;
31      }
32      var gameTimer=setInterval(mainLoop, 10);
33  </script>
34  </html>
```

The **ctx** variable will be used to point to the canvas.

Prepare the variables we will use.

Clear everything from the canvas.

Draw the pipes.

Move the pipes to the left.

Later on, **checkHitPipe** will look for collisions. Stop it for now with //.

If the pipe reaches the left side then move it to the right side, then give it a random **y** value. Increase the score.

Draw the fish.

Set the font style.

Show the score.

Increase how fast the fish falls.

Move the fish down according to how fast it is falling.

Start a game timer that runs quite quickly (100 times a second).

9 Save

In your text editor, click **File > Save**.

File Edit Selection
New File   ctype
Open..   >
Save   id='sc

10 Refresh

Click the **Refresh** button in your web browser.

Try the code

The small fish should appear then fall down to the bottom. Pipes should start moving across the screen. Each time they reach the left, the score should increase.

C documents/fish.html

Score: 3

! Check for errors

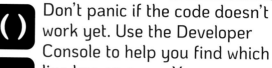

Don't panic if the code doesn't work yet. Use the Developer Console to help you find which line has an error. You may have made a mistake with spelling or capital letters. Check all the symbols are correct on each line. **Save**, **Refresh** and try again!

12 Mind the pipe!

The fish needs to be able to jump up to avoid the pipe. We will add some simple code so that pressing **any** key makes it jump. We need a function to check if the fish hit the pipes — if it has then it's game over.

```
33    document.onkeydown=function(){
34        ySpeed=-2;
35    }
36    function checkHitPipe(){                                    ── Define the function.
37        if(x<70){                                              ── Is the pipe near the fish?
38            if((fishY-y<270)||(fishY-y>450)){                  ── Is it going to hit the fish?
39                clearInterval(gameTimer);                      ── Stop the timer.
40                ctx.font="80px Arial";                         ── Set the font style.
41                ctx.fillText("Game Over!", 100, 250);          ── Show "Game Over!".
42            }                                                  ── End of the second if code.
43        }                                                      ── End of the first if code.
44    }                                                          ── End of the function.
45 </script>
46 </html>
```

```
21              checkHitPipe();
```
Find line 21 and delete the two slashes that were there until the function was ready.

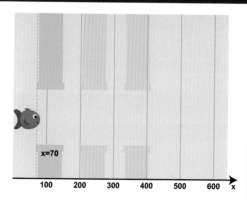

HIT TESTING

To check if the fish hit the pipe we will do two tests.

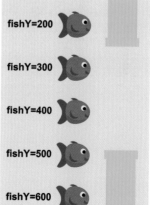

x=70

100 200 300 400 500 600 x

1. Compare their **x** values.

The fish is 80 pixels wide. When the **x** value of the pipe gets to 80 it will just touch the fish. So, check if **x < 70** to make sure it has got really close.

2. Compare their **y** values.

fishY=200
fishY=300
fishY=400
fishY=500
fishY=600

If the difference between the fish and the top of the pipes is less than 270 or more than 450 then they will collide. Our code will test if **fishY-y < 270** or **fishY-y > 450**.

In code, the two vertical lines || mean or.

13 Hide the images

Hide the images that were used to load the graphics. Edit line 6 and set **img** to **display:none**.

```
6        img{display:none;}
```

MAKING COMMENTS

Two slashes at the start of a line of code // tell JavaScript to ignore the whole line.

A line starting with // is called a **comment**. You can use // to stop part of your code running while you are still working on it.

Comments are also used to tell other people what parts of your code do. They are a great way to leave notes in your code about how it works in case you need to alter it later.

14 Save & Refresh

In your text editor, click **File > Save**.

 Refresh the web browser.

15 Test your game

Click the game to give it **focus**. Press any key on the keyboard to make the fish jump. How many pipes can the fish jump through?

documents/fish.html

Score: 12

! Check for errors

If the code doesn't work, check your code, starting with line 38.

Find other bugs with the Developer Console.

See page 31 for help using the Developer Console.

Challenges

- Edit line 20 and change the speed the pipe moves across the screen. You need to make sure you are using a negative number – try -1 or -4.

- Line 23 controls the y position of the pipes on the screen. Experiment with other numbers such as -400 or -200 instead of -320.

- Try changing the font style used at the end of the game. Look at another program on your computer to check which fonts are available.

- Line 29 controls how fast the fish falls down the screen. Try using -0.03 instead of -0.02. What happens? Try other small, negative numbers and experiment!

- Line 34 sets the speed the fish moves up at when it jumps. Type in different values and see how it changes the game. You might need to alter line 29 again if you change line 34, to balance things out.

Here is the complete code for the game.

```
1  <!doctype html>
2  <html>
3  <style>
4      div{width:640px; height:480px;
5          background:url('sea.png');}
6      img{display:none;}
7  </style>
8  <div>
9      <canvas id="gameCanvas" width="640" height="480"></canvas>
10 </div>
11 <img id='fish' src='fish.png'>
12 <img id='pipes' src='pipes.png'>
13 <script>
14     var ctx=gameCanvas.getContext("2d");
15     var x=640, y=-160, fishY=220, ySpeed=0, score=0;
16
17     function mainLoop() {
18         ctx.clearRect(0, 0, 640, 480);
19         ctx.drawImage(pipes,x,y,80,800);
20         x+=-2;
21         checkHitPipe();
22         if(x<-80){
23             x=640; y=Math.random()*-320;
24             score++;
25         }
26         ctx.drawImage(fish,10,fishY,80,80);
27         ctx.font="30px Arial";
28         ctx.fillText("Score: "+score, 10, 30);
29         ySpeed+=0.02;
30         fishY+=ySpeed;
31     }
32     var gameTimer=setInterval(mainLoop, 10);
33     document.onkeydown=function(){
34         ySpeed=-2;
35     }
36     function checkHitPipe(){
37         if(x<70){
38             if((fishY-y<270)||(fishY-y>450)){
39                 clearInterval(gameTimer);
40                 ctx.font="80px Arial";
41                 ctx.fillText("Game Over!", 100, 250);
42             }
43         }
44     }
45 </script>
46 </html>
```

Meteor Storm

Score: 235

Meteor Storm uses some similar ideas to the Dog 'n' Donuts game. Arrays are used to make meteors move across the screen. A rocket positioned on the left side of the screen can be moved up or down to avoid the meteors. Every time the main loop runs, the score will go up.

HOW THE GAME WORKS

All the images needed in the game need to be downloaded before coding.

`score=67`
This variable will store the score for the game.

`rocketY`
`speedY`
These variables store the rocket's position and how fast it is moving up or down.

`x=[]`
`y=[]`
`speed=[]`
The position and speed of the meteors will be kept in **arrays**. These are a bit like lists.

The stars picture will be set as a background for a div. The div will hold the game canvas. The rocket and all the meteors will be drawn onto the canvas.

A timer will run the **mainLoop** function every 20 milliseconds. The **mainLoop** function will then run the **moveMeteors** and **moveRocket** functions.

`moveMeteors()`
This will move all the meteors by using a loop.

`checkForHits()`
This will check how far away a meteor is from the rocket.

When a meteor gets to the left-hand side of the screen it will move to a new random position at the right-hand side.

The **Up** and **Down** arrow keys will set **changeY** to 3 or -3. The **keyPressed** and **moveRocket** functions will then move the rocket up or down.

1 Look for the graphics

Go to **maxw.com/graphics** to find the images you need to make this game.

Use these images to make sure the code works okay. You could try changing some of these later on.

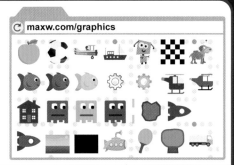

This needs to be the same folder you use to save the HTML game files in this book.

2 Download a rocket

Right-click the rocket.

Choose **Save Image As...**

Open Image in New Tab
Save Image As...
Copy Image
Copy image address

Browse to your Documents folder.

Click **Save**.

Save

3 Download stars and meteors

Repeat Step 2 to download a meteor and the stars background.

4 New file

Open your text editor and start a new file.

File   Edit
New File

5 Save

File   Edit
Save

Save the code as **space.html** in the same folder that you put the images.

6 Start coding

Type in the first part of your code. Include a style section.

```
1 <!doctype html>
2 <html>
3 <style>                                        ← Start of the style section.
4     div{width:640px; height:480px;             ← Set all div elements to be 640 x 480 pixels in
5        background:url('stars.png');}             size and have stars.png as the background.
6    img{display:block;}                          ← Show any images (we will hide them later).
7 </style>                                        ← End of the style section.
8 <div>                                                                              The usual
9    <canvas id="gameCanvas" width="640" height="480"></canvas>  ←  canvas for
10 </div>                                                                             the game.
11 <img id='rocket' src='rocket.png'>  ← The rocket image just downloaded.
12 <img id='meteor' src='meteor.png'>  ← The meteor image.
13 </html>
```

7 View the page

Double-click the **space.html** file.

C | documents/space.html

Scroll down if you can't see all the images.

! Check for errors

If you see this icon instead of one of the three pictures then check you have downloaded them to the correct folder.

Still having problems? Use the Developer Console — see page 31 for help using it.

8 Get moving!

Start adding the JavaScript code. First of all, we will add the variables, including three arrays for the meteors. Add the **mainLoop** function and one to move the meteors.

```
13 <script>
14     var ctx=gameCanvas.getContext("2d");
15     var x=[600,600,600,600,600];
16     var y=[0,100,200,300,400];
17     var speed=[-1,-2,-0.5,-1.2,-1.8];
18     var rocketY=200, changeY=0, score=0;
19
20     var gameTimer=setInterval(mainLoop,20);
21     function mainLoop(){
22         moveMeteors();
23         //moveRocket();
24     }
25     function moveMeteors(){
26         ctx.clearRect(0,0,640,480);
27         for(var n=0; n<5; n++){
28             ctx.drawImage(meteor,x[n],y[n],80,80);
29             x[n]+=speed[n];
30             //checkForHits(n);
31             if(x[n]<-80){
32                 x[n]=640; y[n]=Math.random()*400;
33             }
34         }
35     }
36 </script>
37 </html>
```

*The **ctx** variable will be used when we want to code the canvas.*

*Create three arrays to store the **x**, **y** and **speed** values of each of the meteors.*

Get the other variables ready.

*This runs the **mainLoop** function.*

*The **mainLoop** function runs this code:*

Move all the meteors.

Move the rocket. (We will comment this out so it won't run yet.)

Clear the whole canvas.

Run this code for each meteor:

*Position the meteor at its **x** & **y** values.*

*Move it left by its **speed** value.*

Check if it hit the rocket. (The slashes stop this function running for now.)

If it has reached the left side of the screen then move it to the right.

End of the meteor loop.

9 Save

In the text editor, click **File > Save**.

File Edit Selection
New File
Open.
Save

10 Refresh

Refresh your web browser.

44

The screen should show five meteors. They should keep moving across the screen at different speeds.

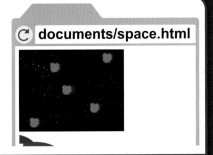

documents/space.html

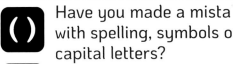
Console.

2 Code the rocket

Next, we need to create a function to move the rocket up or down and write the score on the screen. We will also stop it moving off the screen.

```
36      function moveRocket(){
37          ctx.drawImage(rocket,0,rocketY,80,80);
38          rocketY+=changeY;
39          score+=1;
40          ctx.fillStyle="yellow";
41          ctx.font="30px Arial";
42          ctx.fillText("Score: "+score,10,30);
43          if((rocketY<0)||(rocketY>400)){changeY=0;}
44      }
45 </script>
46 </html>
```

— Draw the rocket on the canvas.
— Move the rocket up or down.
— Change the score.

— Set the font style.

— Show the score.
— If the rocket is too far up or too far down then stop it moving.

```
23              moveRocket();
```
Remove the two slashes from the start of line 23.

3 Save & Refresh

In your text editor, click **File > Save**.

 Refresh the web browser.

14 Test the game

The rocket should now show up on the left and the score should quickly go up.

documents/space.html

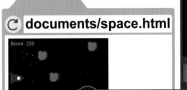

Score: 235

! **Check for errors**

Check for bugs with t Developer Console.

5 Up or down

Add this function to your code so that the arrow keys make it move up or down.

```
45      document.onkeydown=keyPressed;
46      function keyPressed(e){
47          var k=e.keyCode;
48          if(k==38){changeY=-3;}
49          if(k==40){changeY=3;}
50      }
51 </script>
52 </html>
```

← Add a **keydown** listener.
— Define the function.
— Store the key pressed in **k**.

If **Up** was pressed, set **changeY** to **-3**.
If **Down** was pressed, set **changeY** to **3**.

Click **File** > **Save** then **Refresh** the browser.

⁷ Test the code

Click the game to give it **focus**.

Try using the **Up** and **Down** arrow keys to move the rocket.

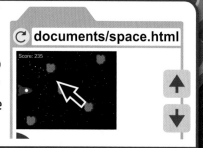

documents/space.html

Score: 235

! Check for errors

If the code doesn't work, check your code. If the rocket goes the wrong way, check you haven't mixed up lines 48 and 49.

Find any bugs with the Developer Console.

³ Up or down

So people can move the rocket up or down, add this function to your code:

```
51        function checkForHits(n){
52            if(Math.abs(x[n]<50)&&
53                (Math.abs(rocketY-y[n])<50)){
54                    clearInterval(gameTimer);
55                    ctx.font="80px Arial";
56                    ctx.fillText("Game Over!",100,250);
57                }
58        }
59 </script>
60 </html>
```

*This function will check if meteor number **n** has hit the rocket.*
Check the horizontal gap.
Now, check the vertical gap.
Stop the timer.
Set the font style.
Show "Game Over!".
*End of the **if** code.*
End of the function.

³ Save & Refresh

Save your code.

 Refresh the browser.

²⁰ Play the game!

The game should now be working!

documents/space.html

Score: 587

! Check for errors

If the code doesn't work, check the last section of code from line 51 to line 60.

> Use the Developer Console to find any bugs.

Challenges

- Edit line 40 to change the colour of the score on the screen.

- The **speed** array in line 17 sets how fast each meteor will move. Try changing some of its values.

- The two large loading images are still shown at the bottom of the page. Edit line 6 to make them invisible.

- Can you add an extra meteor or two? You'll need to edit lines 15, 16, 17 and 27.

- Can you make the meteors smaller? You will also need to alter the code that checks for collisions.

```html
1  <!doctype html>
2  <html>
3  <style>
4      div{width:640px; height:480px;
5          background:url('stars.png');}
6      img{display:block;}
7  </style>
8  <div>
9      <canvas id="gameCanvas" width="640" height="480"></canvas>
10 </div>
11 <img id='rocket' src='rocket.png'>
12 <img id='meteor' src='meteor.png'>
13 <script>
14     var ctx=gameCanvas.getContext("2d");
15     var x=[600,600,600,600,600];
16     var y=[0,100,200,300,400];
17     var speed=[-1,-2,-0.5,-1.2,-1.8];
18     var rocketY=200, changeY=0, score=0;
19
20     var gameTimer=setInterval(mainLoop,20);
21     function mainLoop(){
22         moveMeteors();
23         moveRocket();
24     }
25     function moveMeteors(){
26         ctx.clearRect(0,0,640,480);
27         for(var n=0; n<5; n++){
28             ctx.drawImage(meteor,x[n],y[n],80,80);
29             x[n]+=speed[n];
30             checkForHits(n);
31             if(x[n]<-80){
32                 x[n]=640; y[n]=Math.random()*400;
33             }
34         }
35     }
36     function moveRocket(){
37         ctx.drawImage(rocket,0,rocketY,80,80);
38         rocketY+=changeY;
39         score+=1;
40         ctx.fillStyle="yellow";
41         ctx.font="30px Arial";
42         ctx.fillText("Score: "+score,10,30);
43         if((rocketY<0)||(rocketY>400)){changeY=0;}
44     }
45     document.onkeydown=keyPressed;
46     function keyPressed(e){
47         var k=e.keyCode;
48         if(k==38){changeY=-3;}
49         if(k==40){changeY=3;}
50     }
51     function checkForHits(n){
52         if(Math.abs(x[n]<50)&&
53            (Math.abs(rocketY-y[n])<50)){
54                 clearInterval(gameTimer);
55                 ctx.font="80px Arial";
56                 ctx.fillText("Game Over!",100,250);
57         }
58     }
59 </script>
60 </html>
```

Here is the complete code for the game.

Snake

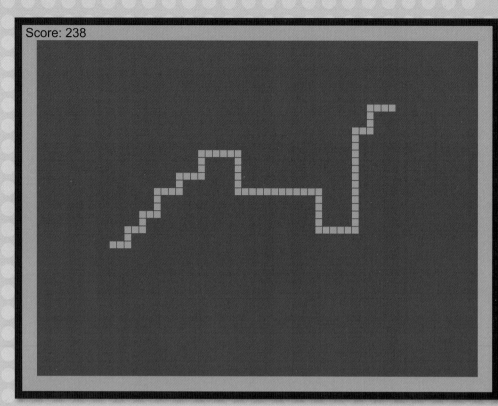

Score: 238

Snake is a classic computer game that became popular on early mobile phones. In our version, we will use the canvas to draw a snake. We use code to find the pixel colour just in front of the snake. This will check if the snake has hit the wall or another part of the snake. If it hits something, the game will stop.

HOW THE GAME WORKS

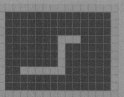

A border will be drawn on the canvas. The snake will be drawn one square at a time using the **fillRect** command.

Two sound effects will be loaded from the web. One will play when a key is pressed, another when the game ends.

A timer will run the **mainLoop** function every 50 milliseconds. It will move the snake forward and increase the score.

The arrow keys will choose the direction the snake will move and store it in the **dir** variable. This will make the snake change its **x** or **y** value.

x=80,y=60
dir=90

These variables store the coordinates of the front of the snake and the direction it is heading.

score=23

This stores the score.

checkForHits()

This function will check if the snake's head has hit the edge or another part of its body.

gameOver() This will stop the game.

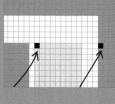

The **checkPixelColour** function will find out which colour the snake is going to hit. It will use the **getImageData** command to do this.

1 Make a new HTML file

Open your text editor or click **File > New File**.

2 Save your file

Click **File > Save**.

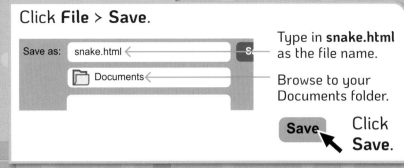

Save as: snake.html

Documents

Save

Type in **snake.html** as the file name.

Browse to your Documents folder.

Click **Save**.

3 Add some code

This part of the code will get the sound effects ready and set up the canvas. A function called **drawBackground** will then draw an orange border on the canvas.

```
1  <!doctype html>
2  <html>
3  <audio id='endMp3' src='https://maxw.com/low.mp3'></audio>
4  <audio id='turnMp3' src='https://maxw.com/high.mp3'></audio>
5  <div style='background-color:blue; height:480px; width:640px;'>
6      <canvas id="gameCanvas" width="640" height="480"></canvas>
7  </div>
8  <script>
9      var ctx=gameCanvas.getContext("2d");
10     var x=240, y=180, dir=90, score=0;
11     drawBackground();
12     function drawBackground(){
13         ctx.strokeStyle='orange';
14         ctx.lineWidth=40;
15         ctx.strokeRect(0, 0, 640, 480);
16     }
17 </script>
18 </html>
```

Prepare the audio elements.

A blue div will show behind the canvas.

The usual ctx variable.

Prepare the variables.

The function to draw the background border.

4 View the page

Double-click the **snake.html** file.

C documents/snake.html

If your page looks like this, go on to Step 5.

! Check for errors

Having problems?

 All the symbols need to be typed correctly. Make sure you typed the code exactly as shown.

 gameCanvas   lineWidth ✓
Gamecanvas   Linewidth ✗

 If you are still stuck then try using the Developer Console.

See page 31 for help using the Developer Console.

5 Make the snake

This code draws the snake a square at a time. The **mainLoop** function will move the square up, down, left or right so that the snake grows and the score increases.

```
17      var gameTimer=setInterval(mainLoop, 50);     ← Start a timer to run the game. It only
18      function mainLoop(){                            needs to run 20 times a second.
19          ctx.fillStyle='orange';                  ← Set the snake's colour.
20          ctx.fillRect(x,y,9,9);                   ← Draw the next square in the snake.
21          if(dir==90){x+=10;}
22          if(dir==180){y+=10;}                       Change the snake's x and y coordinates
23          if(dir==-90){x-=10;}                       depending on which direction it is
24          if(dir==0){y-=10;}                         heading in.
25          //checkPixelColor();                     ← Later, we will check if it has hit something.
26          score++;                                 ← The score increases every loop.
27          ctx.fillRect(0,0,100,20);                ← Clear the space where the score is shown.
28          ctx.fillStyle='black';
29          ctx.font="20px Arial";                     Set the font colour and style.
30          ctx.fillText("Score: "+score,2,16);      ← Show the score.
31      }
32 </script>
33 </html>
```

6 Save

In the text editor, click **File > Save**.

7 Refresh

Refresh your web browser.

8 Test the code

C **documents/snake.html**

Score: 145

The snake should start to move across the screen. It will go through the wall and the score will keep increasing.

(You won't be able to change direction yet.)

Not working?

Check your code!

Are the = + and - signs in lines 21 to 24 all correct?

Aa `fillRect fillStyle` ✓
`fillrect FillStyle` ✗

Use the Developer Console to find any other bugs. **Save**, **Refresh** and test.

HIT TESTING WITH COLOURS

We need to check if the snake's head has hit the border or another part of its body. So, before we move it, we will test the colour of the pixel in front of it.

The **getImageData** command will give us an array (list) of four numbers. These will tell us what colour a particular pixel is.

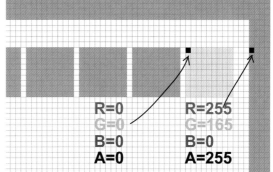

R=0
G=0
B=0
A=0

R=255
G=165
B=0
A=255

The array will contain **R**ed, **G**reen, **B**lue and **A**lpha values.

Line 33 puts this in a variable called **col**. **col**[0] stores R, **col**[1] stores G, and **col**[2] stores the B value. The Alpha part we want is stored in **col**[3].

If the pixel is blank, the A value will be zero. If it's not zero then the pixel is coloured in.

9 Ouch!

If the snake's head bumps into the orange coloured wall or another part of its orange body then it's game over! The next part of the code will deal with this.

```
32      function checkPixelColor(){                        Get the pixel data from where the snake's
33          var col=ctx.getImageData(x,y,1,1).data;         head is. It will contain four values.
34          if(col[3]!=0){                                  If the pixel is not blank, it has hit orange.
35              endMp3.play();                              Play a sound effect.
36              clearInterval(gameTimer);                   Stop the game.
37              ctx.font="80px Arial";                      Set the font style.
38              ctx.fillText("Game Over!",100,250);         Show the "Game Over!" message.
39          }                                               End of the if code.
40      }
41 </script>
42 </html>
```

```
25          checkPixelColor();
```
Find line 25 and delete the comment slashes that were there before the function was ready.

10 Save & Refresh

Save your code.

 Refresh the browser.

11 Test again

The snake should now stop when it hits the orange wall. The score should stop changing.

documents/snake.html
Score: 38

! Check for errors

Having problems? Check the last part of your code from line 32 to line 40. Spot any bugs with the Developer Console.

I can't hear anything!

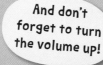
And don't forget to turn the volume up!

NO SOUND?

Playing sounds with code can be tricky. There are lots of special checks browsers make. Some browsers show an error saying "The user didn't interact with the document first". To get around this, refresh the browser then click the game before playing it.

12 Change direction

Finally, we need to make the snake move up, down, left or right when the arrow keys are pressed.

```
41      document.onkeydown=handleKey;
42      function handleKey(e){
43          var k=e.keyCode;
44          if(k==38){dir=0;}
45          if(k==39){dir=90;}
46          if(k==40){dir=180;}
47          if(k==37){dir=-90;}
48          turnMp3.currentTime=0;
49          turnMp3.play();
50      }
```

Add a keyboard listener.
Define the function.
Store the key code.

Set the direction in which the snake will move, based on which arrow key is pressed.

Rewind the sound effect.

Play the sound effect.

WHICH WAY?

This function will work out the direction in which the snake has to go. It will store it in the **dir** variable.

dir=0

38

37   39

dir=-90   dir=90

40

dir=180

13 Save & Refresh

Save your code.   **Refresh** the browser.

14 Try the game!

Your game should now be working! Guide the snake around the screen. How many points can you score?

documents/snake.html

Score: 54

! Check for errors

Having problems? Check the last part of your code. If the arrow keys make the snake go in the wrong direction, check lines 44 to 47. Still stuck? Use the Developer Console.

Click the game to give it focus at the start.

Click Refresh to play the game again.

Challenges

- Find the lines that set the colour of the background, the border and the snake. Experiment with different colours for each of them.

- Line 17 controls how often the **mainLoop** function runs. Try out different values to make the game faster or slower.

- Try to find some other sound effects on your computer and use them instead.

- Line 20 draws each square section of the snake. Instead of making it 9 x 9 pixels, try to make it 10 x 10 or 8 x 8.

- Look at another program on your computer to see which fonts are available. Try changing the font style used at the end of the game and for the score.

```
1  <!doctype html>
2  <html>
3  <audio id='endMp3' src='https://maxw.com/low.mp3'></audio>
4  <audio id='turnMp3' src='https://maxw.com/high.mp3'></audio>
5  <div style='background-color:blue; height:480px; width:640px;'>
6      <canvas id="gameCanvas" width="640" height="480"></canvas>
7  </div>
8  <script>
9      var ctx=gameCanvas.getContext("2d");
10     var x=240, y=180, dir=90, score=0;
11     drawBackground();
12     function drawBackground(){
13         ctx.strokeStyle='orange';
14         ctx.lineWidth=40;
15         ctx.strokeRect(0, 0, 640, 480);
16     }
17     var gameTimer=setInterval(mainLoop, 50);
18     function mainLoop(){
19         ctx.fillStyle='orange';
20         ctx.fillRect(x,y,9,9);
21         if(dir==90){x+=10;}
22         if(dir==180){y+=10;}
23         if(dir==-90){x-=10;}
24         if(dir==0){y-=10;}
25         checkPixelColor();
26         score++;
27         ctx.fillRect(0,0,100,20);
28         ctx.fillStyle='black';
29         ctx.font="20px Arial";
30         ctx.fillText("Score: "+score,2,16);
31     }
32     function checkPixelColor(){
33         var col=ctx.getImageData(x,y,1,1).data;
34         if(col[3]!=0){
35             endMp3.play();
36             clearInterval(gameTimer);
37             ctx.font="80px Arial";
38             ctx.fillText("Game Over!",100,250);
39         }
40     }
41     document.onkeydown=handleKey;
42     function handleKey(e){
43         var k=e.keyCode;
44         if(k==38){dir=0;}
45         if(k==39){dir=90;}
46         if(k==40){dir=180;}
47         if(k==37){dir=-90;}
48         turnMp3.currentTime=0;
49         turnMp3.play();
50     }
51  </script>
52  </html>
```

Here is the complete code for the game.

Break Wall

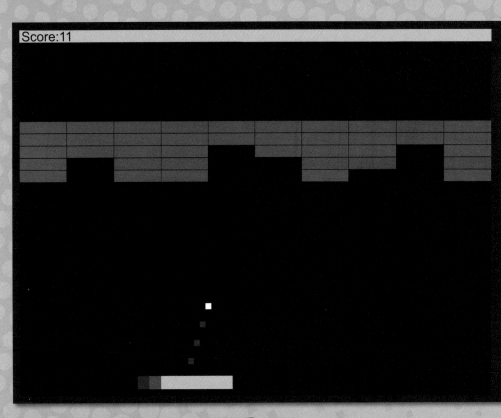

Score:11

The bricks in this game will be drawn onto the canvas using code. A ball will be drawn on the canvas, then erased after it moves. The code will check the pixel colour where the ball is. If it hits a brick, it will clear it from the canvas. The bat will move when the mouse moves.

HOW THE GAME WORKS

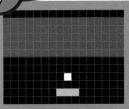

Bricks, a bat and a ball will be drawn on the canvas. We will use colour codes to change the shade of the bricks.

x,y — These store the ball's coordinates.

speedX **speedY** — These store how fast the ball moves horizontally and vertically.

batX — The x value of the bat.

score — This variable stores the score.

If the ball hits the side, we will make it bounce by setting *speedX* to be minus *speedX*.

If it hits the top, we will change the *speedY* variable.

The bat will move left or right to match the x position of the mouse.

A timer will run the **mainLoop** function every 25 milliseconds. It will move the ball forward.

A ping sound effect will be loaded from the web. It will play when the ball hits a brick.

drawBricks() — Two loops will draw the bricks onto the canvas.

checkForHits() — This will check if the ball hits a brick or the bat.

gameOver() — This will stop the game.

The **checkPixelColour** function will find out if the ball is going to hit a brick. It will use the **getImageData** command to do this.

1 Make a new HTML file

Open your text editor or click **File > New File**.

2 Save

Click **Save** and use **wall.html** as the file name.

Save → Save the code in your Documents folder.

3 Start coding!

This part of the code will get the sound effects ready, and set up the canvas. A function called **drawBackground** will then draw an orange border on the canvas.

```
1  <!doctype html>
2  <html>
3  <audio id='pingMp3' src='https://maxw.com/ping.mp3'></audio>     ← Prepare the audio.
4  <div style='background-color:#333333; width:640px;'>              ┐ A dark grey div
5      <canvas id="gameCanvas" width="640" height="480"></canvas>   ├ will show behind
6  </div>                                                           ┘ the canvas.
7  <script>                                                          ┐ The usual ctx
8      var ctx=gameCanvas.getContext("2d");            ←             ┘ variable.
9      var x=280, y=400, speedX=0, speedY=-8, batX=280, score=0;  ─ The variables.
10     drawBricks();                    \                            ┐ The function to
11     function drawBricks(){ /                                      ┘ draw the bricks.
12         for(a=0; a<5; a++){                         \             ┐ Repeat 5 rows of
13             for(b=0; b<8; b++){ /                                  ┘ 8 columns.
14                 ctx.fillStyle='#ff00'+(40+a*40).toString(16); ←  Set the colour.
15                 ctx.fillRect(b*80,100+a*20,79,19); ←             Draw each brick.
16             } ←                                                   End of loop b.
17         } ←                                                       End of loop a.
18     } ←                                                           End of the
19  </script>                                                         function.
20  </html>
```

1, 2, 3...

a * b

DRAWING BRICKS WITH LOOPS

We need to draw 40 bricks in this game. If each brick had its own code it would take a lot of time to type!

Instead, we will use two loops. The first will loop through each of the five rows. The second will loop through each of the eight columns. Each loop will start counting at 0.

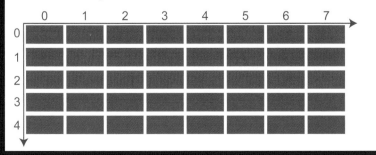

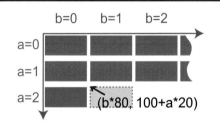

To position each block, we have to do some quite tricky maths. To get the x position, we can multiply **b** by 80. To get the y value, we multiply **a** by 20 and add 100 to leave space at the top of the canvas.

Save

In the text editor, click **File > Save**.

File   Edit   Selection

New File
Open..
Save

5 **View the page**

Double-click the **wall.html** file.

C **documents/wall.html**

All the bricks should be drawn like this.

! **Check for errors**

If your screen doesn't look like this, check:

<> All the symbols are typed correctly. Make sure you typed the code exactly as shown.

Aa   gameCanvas drawBricks ✓
     Gamecanvas DrawBricks ✗

() If you are still stuck then try using the Developer Console.

See Page 31 for a reminder.

6 **Move the ball**

Now, we need to get the ball moving. Our code will make sure the ball bounces off the side walls and the top. It will also move the bat by setting its x coordinate to the value of **batX**.

```
19        var gameTimer=setInterval(mainLoop, 25);    ← Start a timer to run the game.
20·       function mainLoop() {
21            ctx.clearRect(x,y,7,7);                 ← Clear the place where the ball was.
22            x=x+speedX;                             ← Change its x value by speedX.
23            y=y+speedY;                             ← Change its y value by speedY.
24            //checkForHits();                       ← Later, this will check if any bricks have been hit.
25            ctx.fillStyle='#ffffff';                ← Set white as the colour to draw the ball.
26            ctx.fillRect(x,y,7,7);                  ← Draw the ball.
27            if((x>620)||(x<0))speedX=-speedX;       ← If it has hit the left or right wall, make it bounce.
28            if(y<28)speedY=8;                       ← Make it bounce off the top of the screen.
29            //if(y>480){gameOver();}                ← Check if it has gone past the bat.
30            ctx.clearRect(0,460,640,20);            ← Clear the space where the bat might be.
31            ctx.fillStyle='#cccccc';                ← Set the colour to light grey.
32            ctx.fillRect(batX-60,460,120,20);       ← Draw the bat.
33        }
34 </script>
35 </html>
```

7 **Save & Refresh**

Save your code.   C   **Refresh** the browser.

8 Test your code

The ball should travel through the bricks, bounce off the top and disappear.

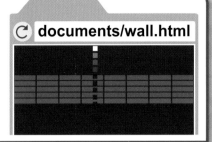

documents/wall.html

! Check for errors

Code not working? Check all the code from line 19 onwards.

If you are still having problems, use the Developer Console.

9 Check for hits

This next function deals with the bat hitting the bat or one of the bricks. If it hits the bat, we need to work out which angle to send it back at. If it hits a brick, we need to work out which one it was.

```
34      function checkForHits(){
35          var col=ctx.getImageData(x,y,1,1).data;
36          if((y>460)&&(Math.abs(batX-x)<60)){
37              speedY=-8;
38              speedX=Math.round(0.15*(x-batX));
39          }else if(col[3]!=0){
40              pingMp3.currentTime=0;
41              pingMp3.play();
42              var x0=80*Math.floor(x/80);
43              var y0=20*Math.floor(y/20);
44              ctx.clearRect(x0,y0,79,19);
45              speedY=-speedY;
46              score++;
47              ctx.fillRect(0,0,640,20);
48              ctx.fillStyle='black';
49              ctx.font="20px Arial";
50              ctx.fillText("Score: "+score,2,16);
51          }
52      }
53 </script>
54 </html>
```

Get the pixel data from where the ball is. It will contain four numbers.
If the ball is touching the bat then:
Make it move upwards.
Set how fast it moves sideways.
If it's not touching the bat, check if it hit a brick.
If it did hit one then rewind the sound.
Play the sound effect.
Calculate the x and y coordinates of the brick that the ball has hit.
Erase the brick.
Change the vertical direction of the ball.
Increase the score by 1.
Clear the screen where the score was.
Set the font style for the score.
Show the score.

```
24          checkForHits();
```

Go to line 24 and delete the two slashes that were there until this function was ready.

This is how line 38 decides which way the ball will bounce.

BOUNCE ANGLES

If the ball hits the bat on its left-hand side, we want the ball to bounce off to the left.

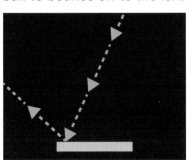

If the ball hits the bat exactly in the middle, then it should bounce straight up.

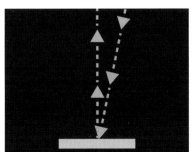

If it touches the bat on the right-hand side, it needs to bounce off to the right.

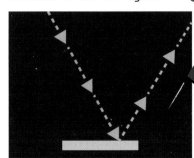

10 Save & Refresh

Save your code. **Refresh** the browser.

11 Test your code

The ball should bounce between the bat and the bricks, knocking out one brick each time. The score should go up. (You can't move the bat yet.)

documents/wall.html

Score: 3

! Check for errors

Check all the code from line 34 onwards.

Use the Developer Console to help.

12 Game Over!

Lastly, add code to make the bat move, and make the **gameOver** function.

```
53     document.onmousemove=function(){batX=event.clientX;}
54     function gameOver(){
55         clearInterval(gameTimer); ←
56         ctx.font="80px Arial"; ←
57         ctx.fillText("Game Over!", 100, 250); ←
58     }
59 </script>
60 </html>
```

*When the mouse moves, set **batX** to the mouse x value.*

Stop the timer.

Set the font style.

Show the "Game Over!" message.

```
29             if(y>480){gameOver();}
```
In line 29, delete the two slashes so that the code runs.

13 Save & Refresh

Save your code.

 Refresh the browser.

14 Try your game!

You should be able to move the bat with the mouse and control where the ball goes. See how many bricks you can smash!

documents/wall.html

Score: 11

! Not working?

Click the game to give it **focus**.

Check your code from line 53 onwards.

Still stuck? Use the Developer Console.

Challenges

- Speed up or slow down the game by changing the timer value in line 19.
- Can you change the colours? See page 77 for help with colour codes.
- In line 14, replace 40 with 20. What happens? Experiment!
- Change the number of rows drawn to 6, 7 or even more...

```html
1  <!doctype html>
2  <html>
3  <audio id='pingMp3' src='https://maxw.com/ping.mp3'></audio>
4  <div style='background-color:#333333; width:640px;'>
5      <canvas id="gameCanvas" width="640" height="480"></canvas>
6  </div>
7  <script>
8      var ctx=gameCanvas.getContext("2d");
9      var x=280, y=400, speedX=0, speedY=-8, batX=280, score=0;
10     drawBricks();
11     function drawBricks(){
12         for(a=0; a<5; a++){
13             for(b=0; b<8; b++){
14                 ctx.fillStyle='#ff00'+(40+a*40).toString(16);
15                 ctx.fillRect(b*80,100+a*20,79,19);
16             }
17         }
18     }
19     var gameTimer=setInterval(mainLoop, 25);
20     function mainLoop() {
21         ctx.clearRect(x,y,7,7);
22         x=x+speedX;
23         y=y+speedY;
24         checkForHits();
25         ctx.fillStyle='#ffffff';
26         ctx.fillRect(x,y,7,7);
27         if((x>620)||(x<0))speedX=-speedX;
28         if(y<28)speedY=8;
29         if(y>480){gameOver();}
30         ctx.clearRect(0,460,640,20);
31         ctx.fillStyle='#cccccc';
32         ctx.fillRect(batX-60,460,120,20);
33     }
34     function checkForHits(){
35         var col=ctx.getImageData(x,y,1,1).data;
36         if((y>460)&&(Math.abs(batX-x)<60)){
37             speedY=-8;
38             speedX=Math.round(0.15*(x-batX));
39         }else if(col[3]!=0){
40             pingMp3.currentTime=0;
41             pingMp3.play();
42             var x0=80*Math.floor(x/80);
43             var y0=20*Math.floor(y/20);
44             ctx.clearRect(x0,y0,79,19);
45             speedY=-speedY;
46             score++;
47             ctx.fillRect(0,0,640,20);
48             ctx.fillStyle='black';
49             ctx.font="20px Arial";
50             ctx.fillText("Score: "+score,2,16);
51         }
52     }
53     document.onmousemove=function(){batX=event.clientX;}
54     function gameOver(){
55         clearInterval(gameTimer);
56         ctx.font="80px Arial";
57         ctx.fillText("Game Over!", 100, 250);
58     }
59  </script>
60  </html>
```

Here is the complete code for the game.

Game Challenge: Simple Catching

If you have coded Catch It! then you are ready to try coding this game.

Score: 12

In this project you will get the chance to design your own simple catching game. You can pick your own images and download them to use in the game. The code will be very similar to Catch It! but you will need to adapt it to include your images. What other changes will you make?

Choose what your player image will be. Perhaps an animal or a monster?

A dog?

What will you be catching? Something to eat, maybe?

In the code we will call these the player and the food.

HOW THE GAME WORKS

All the images for the game need to be chosen and downloaded before coding.

score=3 The score variable will count how many things have been caught.

x,y These store the falling object's coordinates.

Copies of the player image and the falling object will be drawn onto the canvas using the **drawImage** command.

playerX changeX These hold the **x** value of the player, and how much it should move.

checkForHits() This function will check if the player is near enough to the object to eat it.

A timer will run the **mainLoop** function every 20 milliseconds. It will move the object down and show the score so far.

A second timer will stop the game after 30 seconds.

gameOver() This will stop the game.

If the falling object gets to the bottom of the screen or gets eaten, it will move to a new random position at the top.

The **Left** and **Right** arrow keys will set **changeX** to be 4 or -4 (minus 4). This makes the player move left or right.

Go online and search for the first image you want to use. If you are looking for a cupcake, try searching for **cupcake clipart**.

 cupcake clipart

Click on one of the images.

Sometimes, it helps if you add the word "transparent" to your search.

Find the large version of the image.

Right-click the image.

Choose **Save Image As...**

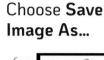

Open Image in New Tab
Save Image As..
Copy Image
Copy image address

Rename the image.

Save as:	cupcake.png	**Save**

📁 Documents ◄

Don't save it in your Downloads folder. Browse to the Documents folder you use for the HTML files in this book.

catch.html
space.html
donuts.html

Save ◄ Click **Save**.

Repeat Steps 1 to 3 to download another image.

Open Image in New Tab
Save Image As..
Copy Image
Copy image address

You need to save your HTML file in the same folder you put the images in.

File Edit
New File ◄

Open your text editor and click **File > New File**.

Click **Save** and choose a suitable name for your game.

Save as:	mygame1.html ◄	Sa

📁 Documents

catch.html
cupcake.html

*The name must end with **.html***

Save ◄ Click **Save**.

Type in all the code for your game. See pages 21 to 25 to find out more about what
each line of code does. The line numbers match, and most of the code is the same.

Choose your own background colour – see page 77.

Type in one of your downloaded image file names.

Use the other downloaded image file name.

How fast do you want the object to fall?

Remember to keep saving your work every few minutes!

How quickly will the player move?

Choose key codes for the keys you want to use (see page 24).

Choose how many points each object will get.

How long do you want the game to last?

Pick your own message at the end of the game.

```
1  <!doctype html>
2  <html>
3  <div style='background-color:MediumOrchid; width:640px;'>
4      <canvas id="gameCanvas" width="640" height="480"></canvas>
5  </div>
6  <div style='display:none;'>
7      <img id='food' src='cupcake.png'>
8      <img id='player' src='pm.png'>
9  </div>
10 <script>
11     var ctx=gameCanvas.getContext("2d");
12     var x=300, y=50, playerX=300, changeX=0, score=0;
13
14     var gameTimer=setInterval(mainLoop,20);
15     function mainLoop() {
16         ctx.clearRect(0,0,640,480);
17         ctx.font="30px Arial";
18         ctx.fillText("Score: "+score,10,30);
19         ctx.drawImage(food,x,y,80,80);
20         y+=3;
21         if(y>480){y=-80; x=Math.random()*600;}
22         ctx.drawImage(player,playerX,400,80,80);
23         playerX+=changeX;
24         checkForHits();
25     }
26     document.onkeydown=keyPressed;
27     function keyPressed(e){
28         var k=e.keyCode;
29         if(k==37){changeX=-4;}
30         if(k==39){changeX=4;}
31     }
32     function checkForHits(){
33         if((Math.abs(400-y)<60)&&
34             (Math.abs(playerX-x)<60)){
35             score+=1;
36             y=-80; x=Math.random()*600;
37         }
38     }
39     setTimeout(gameOver,30000);
40     function gameOver(){
41         clearInterval(gameTimer);
42         ctx.font="80px Arial";
43         ctx.fillText("Game Over!",100,250);
44     }
45 </script>
46 </html>
```

8 Save & Refresh

Save your code. **Refresh** the browser.

9 Test your game

The game should now be fully working. How many points can you get before the time is up?

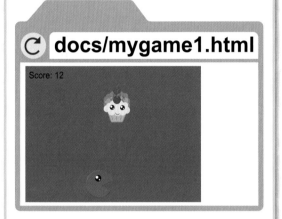

docs/mygame1.html

Score: 12

! Check for errors

Problems? Check your code very carefully, then **Save** and **Refresh**.

Aa gameOver fillText gameTimer ✓
GameOver fillText Gametimer ✗

📁 If the images aren't showing up, check you have put them in the correct folder and spelt their file names correctly.

( ) *+ { } Make sure you have typed all the code and symbols correctly.

If the game still isn't working, open up the Developer Console and look for any bugs.

See page 31 for help on using the Developer Console.

 Click Refresh to play the game again.

Cake..!

Challenges

- Experiment with the code inside the yellow lines.
- Find the mods section on page 72.
  - Add some instructions.
  - Experiment with the colours.
  - Draw your own images for the game.
  - Add screen boundaries to stop the player moving off screen.

Game Challenge: Avoiding Games

If you have coded Meteor Storm then you are ready to try coding this game.

Score: 12

How about designing your own game where the player has to dodge and avoid moving objects? You can choose your own images and download them for use in the game. The code will be very similar to Meteor Storm but you will need to edit it to use your own images and make other changes.

Choose what your player image will be. Maybe a car, a submarine or a plane?

A dog?

Pick what you will be dodging – perhaps a monster, a shark or a cloud?

In the code we will call these images the player and the wall – as it will block the player.

HOW THE GAME WORKS

All the images needed in the game need to be downloaded before coding.

score=67 This variable will store the score for the game.

playerY speedY These variables store the player's position and how fast it is moving up or down.

**x=[ ]
y=[ ]
speed=[ ]** The position and speed of the walls (or clouds) will be kept in arrays.

One of your downloaded pictures will be set as the background for a div. The div will hold the game canvas. Everything else will be drawn on the canvas.

A timer will run the **mainLoop** function every 20 milliseconds. The **mainLoop** function will then run the **moveWalls** and **movePlayer** functions.

moveWalls() This will move all the walls by using a loop.

checkForHits() This will check how far away a cloud is from the player.

When a wall gets to the left-hand side of the screen it will move to a new random position at the right-hand side.

The **Up** and **Down** arrow keys will set **changeY** to 3 or -3. The **keyPressed** and **movePlayer** functions will then move the player up or down.

1 Look for your graphics

Go online and search for the images you need. If you are looking for a biplane, try searching for **biplane clipart**.

 **biplane clipart**

2 Choose an image

Click on one of the images.

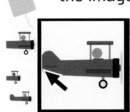

You will get more useful images if you add "transparent" to your search.

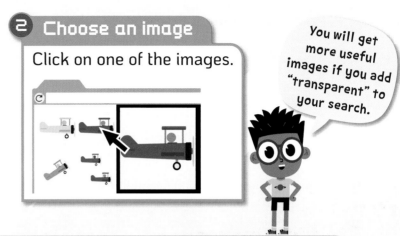

3 Download it

Find the large version of the image.

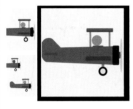

Right-click the image.

Choose **Save Image As...**

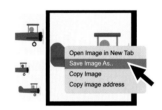

Rename the image.

Save as:	biplane.png	**Save**
	📁 Documents
	catch.html
	space.html
	donuts.html

Don't save it in your Downloads folder. Save it in the Documents folder you used for the HTML files in this book.

Save Click **Save**.

4 Download another image

Repeat Steps 1 to 3 to download something to dodge and a background.

 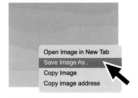

You need to save your HTML file in the same folder you put the images in.

5 Make a new HTML file

File	Edit
New File	

Open your text editor and click **File > New File**.

6 Save

Click **Save** and choose a suitable name for your game.

Save as:	mygame2.html	**Sav**
	📁 Documents
	catch.html
	cupcake.html

The name must end with .html

Save Click **Save**.

See pages 42 to 45 to find out more about what each line of code does. The line numbers match.

```
1  <!doctype html>
2  <html>
3  <style>
4      div{width:640px; height:480px;
5          background:url('sky.png');}
6      img{display:none;}
7  </style>
8  <div>
9      <canvas id="gameCanvas" width="640" height="480"></canvas>
10 </div>
11 <img id='player' src='biplane.png'>
12 <img id='wall' src='cloud.png'>
13 <script>
14     var ctx=gameCanvas.getContext("2d");
15     var x=[600,600,600,600,600];
16     var y=[0,100,200,300,400];
17     var speed=[-1,-2,-0.5,-1.2,-1.8];
18     var playerY=200, changeY=0, score=0;
19
20     var gameTimer=setInterval(mainLoop,20);
21     function mainLoop(){
22         moveWalls();
23         movePlayer();
24     }
25     function moveWalls(){
26         ctx.clearRect(0,0,640,480);
27         for(var n=0; n<5; n++){
28             ctx.drawImage(wall,x[n],y[n],80,80);
29             x[n]+=speed[n];
30             checkForHits(n);
31             if(x[n]<-80){
32                 x[n]=640; y[n]=Math.random()*400;
33             }
34         }
35     }
36     function movePlayer(){
37         ctx.drawImage(player,0,playerY,80,80);
38         playerY+=changeY;
39         score+=1;
40         ctx.fillStyle="yellow";
41         ctx.font="30px Arial";
42         ctx.fillText("Score: "+score,10,30);
43         if((playerY<0)||(playerY>400)){changeY=0;}
44     }
45     document.onkeydown=keyPressed;
46     function keyPressed(e){
47         var k=e.keyCode;
48         if(k==38){changeY=-3;}
49         if(k==40){changeY=3;}
50     }
51     function checkForHits(n){
52         if(Math.abs(x[n]<40)&&
53             (Math.abs(playerY-y[n])<40)){
54                 clearInterval(gameTimer);
55                 ctx.font="80px Arial";
56                 ctx.fillText("Game Over!",100,250);
57         }
58     }
59 </script>
60 </html>
```

Use the file name of the downloaded background image.

Use the player image file name.

Use the other downloaded image file name.

How fast will the game be?

Keep saving your work every few minutes!

Choose how many points each object will get.

How quickly will the player move?

Choose key codes for the keys you want to use (see page 24).

Pick a message to show at the end of your game.

Save & Refresh

Save your code. **Refresh** the browser.

Test your game

Your game should now be working. See how long you can keep playing before you hit something!

⟳ **docs/mygame2.html**

! Check for errors

Problems? Check the last few lines of your code carefully, then **Save** and **Refresh**.

 mainLoop drawImage moveWalls ✓
mainloop DrawImage movewalls ✗

 If you can't see all of the pictures, check you have put them in the right folder and spelt the file names correctly.

   Check you have typed all the code and symbols correctly.

If you are still having problems, open up the Developer Console and look for any bugs.

See page 31 for help on using the Developer Console.

 Click Refresh to play the game again.

Look out!

 Change my x value!

Challenges

- Experiment with the code inside the yellow lines.
- Find the mods section on page 72.
  - Add some instructions for your game. This will also give it "focus".
  - Experiment with the colour of the text.
  - Draw your own images for the game.
  - Add a high score to the game.

Game Challenge: Advanced Catching

> If you have coded Dog 'n' Donuts then you are ready to try coding this game.

Score: 7

In this activity you will design a more advanced catching game. You will need to download some images that will scroll across the page. The player has to collect as many as they can. A sound effect will play and the score will go up with every one caught. This game uses very similar code to Dog 'n' Donuts, but the objects will move horizontally across the page.

> Choose what your player image will be. Maybe a whale or a submarine?

> Pick what you will be collecting. It could be a star, a heart or some food.

> In the code we will call these images the player and the star.

HOW THE GAME WORKS

 All the images for the game need to be picked and downloaded before coding.

`x=[]`
`y=[]`
`speed=[]`
The position and speed of the objects (stars) will be kept in arrays.

 A timer will run the **mainLoop** function every 20 milliseconds. It will move the objects sideways and show the score so far.

 Each object (star) will move to a new random position at the right-hand side after they reach the left-hand side or get eaten.

`score=8` This variable will count how many objects get eaten.

`playerY=30` This will store the y position of the player.

 A sound effect will play when an object is caught. It will be loaded from a website.

`checkForHits()` This function will check how far away a particular object is from the player.

`gameOver()` This will stop the game.

 The **Up** and **Down** arrow keys will set **changeY** to be 4 or -4. This will move the player up or down. The **keyPressed** function will make this work.

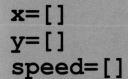

1 Look for your graphics

Go online and search for the first image you want to use. If you are looking for a submarine, try searching for **submarine clipart**.

 submarine clipart

2 Choose an image

Click on one of the images.

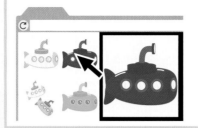

Sometimes it helps if you add the word "transparent" to your search.

3 Download it

Find the large version of the image.

Right-click the image.

Choose **Save Image As...**

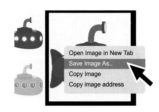

Rename the image.

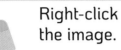

Save as: | sub.png | **Save**
Documents ←

catch.html
space.html
donuts.html

Don't save it in your Downloads folder. Browse to the Documents folder you use for the HTML files in this book.

Save Click **Save**.

4 Download another image

Repeat Steps 1 to 3 to download another image.

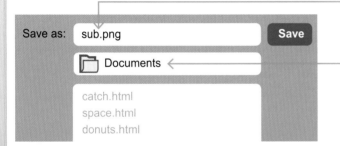

5 Make a new HTML file

Open your text editor and click **File > New File**.

File   Edit
New File

6 Save

Click **Save** and choose a suitable name for your game.

Save as: | mygame3.html ← | Sa
Documents

catch.html
cupcake.html

The name must end with .html

Save Click **Save**.

You need to save your HTML file in the same folder you put the images in.

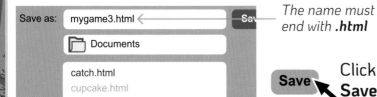

See pages 29 to 35 to find out more about what each line of code does. The line numbers match.

Save your work every few minutes!

```html
1  <!doctype html>
2  <html>
3  <audio id='beep' src='https://maxw.com/beep2.mp3'></audio>
4  <div style='background-color:Aquamarine; width:640px;'>
5      <canvas id="gameCanvas" width="640" height="480"></canvas>
6  </div>
7  <div style='display:none;'>
8      <img id='player' src='sub.png'>
9      <img id='star' src='star.png'>
10 </div>
11 <script>
12     var ctx=gameCanvas.getContext("2d");
13     var x=[640,640,640,640,640,640,640];
14     var y=[0,50,100,200,300,350,400];
15     var speed=[-2,-1,-3,-1.5,-2.5,-3.5,-2];
16     var playerY=300, changeY=0, score=0;
17
18     var gameTimer=setInterval(mainLoop,20);
19     function mainLoop(){
20         ctx.clearRect(0,0,640,480);
21         ctx.font="30px Arial";
22         ctx.fillText("Score: "+score,10,30);
23         for(var n=0; n<7; n++){
24             ctx.drawImage(star,x[n],y[n],40,40);
25             x[n]+=speed[n];
26             checkForHits(n);
27             if(x[n]<-80){
28                 x[n]=640; y[n]=Math.random()*400;
29             }
30         }
31         ctx.drawImage(player,0,playerY,80,80);
32         playerY+=changeY;
33     }
34     document.onkeydown=keyPressed;
35     function keyPressed(e){
36         var k=e.keyCode;
37         if(k==38){changeY=-4;}
38         if(k==40){changeY=4;}
39     }
40     function checkForHits(n){
41         if((Math.abs(x[n])<50)&&
42             (Math.abs(playerY-y[n])<50)){
43             score+=1;
44             x[n]=640; y[n]=Math.random()*400;
45             beep.play();
46         }
47     }
48     setTimeout(gameOver,60000);
49     function gameOver(){
50         clearInterval(gameTimer);
51         ctx.font="80px Arial";
52         ctx.fillText("Game Over!",100,250);
53     }
54 </script>
55 </html>
```

If you have an mp3 file of your own, change this part of the code.

Use the player image file name.

Use the other downloaded file name.

Choose how fast will the game will run.

Set the number of stars

Set the size of the stars.

Set how fast the player will move up and down.

Choose key codes for the keys you want to use (see page 24).

Choose how many points each object will get.

Set how long each game will last.

Choose text to show at the end of the game.

8 Save & Refresh

Save your code. **Refresh** the browser.

9 Test your game

The game should now be working. How many stars can you collect before your time is up?

docs/mygame3.html

Score: 7

! Check for errors

Problems? Check the last few lines of your code carefully, then **Save** and **Refresh**.

 mainLoop clearRect drawImage ✓
mainloop clearRECT Drawimage ✗

 If you can't see some of the pictures, check you have put them in the correct folder and typed the file names properly.

   Make sure you have typed all the code and symbols correctly.

If the code is still not working, open up the Developer Console and look for bugs.

See page 31 for help on using the Developer Console.

 Click Refresh to play the game again.

I'm seeing stars..!

Challenges

- Experiment with the code inside the yellow lines.

- Add two more stars to the screen. Make the **x,y** and **speed** arrays longer and change the number of times the loop runs in line 23.

- Find the mods section on page 72.

  - Add some instructions for your game.

  - Add some boundaries to stop the submarine going off the screen.

  - Draw your own images for the game.

  - Add a high score to the game.

Game Mods

After you have coded a game and tried the challenges there are still lots of extra things you can add to make your game even better! In this section there are some exciting ways to modify your games. Experiment and have fun with your code.

Before you start using this section, load a game you have finished coding. Then, choose one of the mods to use.

> Mods are ways to change a game. Mods is short for modifications.

A) Instructions

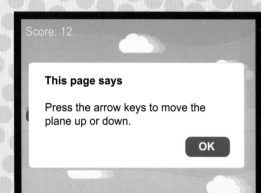

Here is a simple mod that you can use in all games. It displays a short sentence as an instruction panel. The player has to click OK to start the game.

This has the added bonus of setting focus – making sure that the game is "listening" for any key presses.

> Insert the code that's inside the dotted yellow box.

A1 Add an alert

Find the line before the end of the script. Press **Enter** to make some space, and insert the following line:

```
    alert('Use the arrow keys to move the plane up or down.');
</script>
```

Type instructions for your game between the quotes.

Save your file and **Refresh** the browser to test your code.

B) Screen Boundary

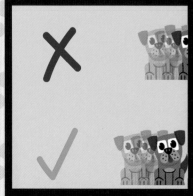

In most of the games in this book, the player moves left and right or up and down. But sometimes, the player can move off the screen.

To stop that, we can add some code. We need to check the x or y position and limit it if it gets too big or too small.

Add the code that's inside the dotted yellow box.

B1 Add some checks

Look inside the **mainLoop** function in your game.

```
dogX+=changeX;
if(dogX<0)dogX=0;
if(dogX>560)dogX=560;
```

— *Find the code where the player, the monster or the dog is moved.*
Add this code to check if it has reached the left-hand side of the screen.

Insert this line to test if it has got near the right-hand side.

Save your file and **Refresh** the browser to test your code.

 If you are modding **Catch It!**, use **monsterX** instead of **dogX**.

 If you are modding your own game from the code on page 60, use **playerX** instead of **dogX**.

 If you are modding your own game from page 64 or page 68, use **playerY** instead of **dogX** and use 400 instead of 560.

C) High Score

Score: 235   High Score: 235

In this mod you will add a high score to your code so that it keeps track of the best score anyone has managed in your game.

If we used a normal variable to store the high score it would get reset when you reloaded a page. Instead, we will use "local storage" – this is stored more permanently in your browser.

C1 Set up your variables

Add these lines after the other variables are set up near the start of your code after the **var** commands:

```
var highScore=0, loc=localStorage.getItem('highScore');
if(loc>0)highScore=loc;
```

This code gets the current high score from local storage.

Save your file.

C2 Show the high score

Find the part of your code where the score is shown, and add this line below it:

```
ctx.fillText("Score: "+score,10,30);
ctx.fillText("High Score: "+highScore,400,30);
```

Show the high score on the right of the screen.

Save your file.

Update the high score if it has been beaten

Find where "Game Over!" is shown near the end of your code, and insert these lines:

```
ctx.fillText("Game Over!",100,250);
if(score>highScore){
    localStorage.setItem('highScore',score);
}
```

Check if the current score is better than the old high score. If it is then store it in the local storage.

Save your file and **Refresh** the browser to test your code.

Use the Developer Console to find any errors.

D) Creating Images

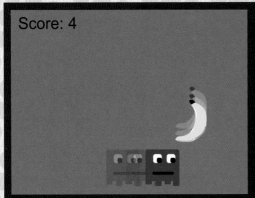

Score: 4

In the game challenges you learned how to download your own choice of image and add it to a game.

Another way to make your own games is to draw the images using a painting program. These can then be added to your game.

D1 Start a painting program

There are hundreds of painting programs you can use to make images. We just need a simple one for this. If you are using a Windows computer, find the **Paint** program and start it. Alternatively, there are various online painting programs you can use. Search for **online paint** to find a simple one.

🔄 **jspaint.app**

File Edit View Image

D2 Image attributes

Use the menu to bring up the image attributes — the settings for the picture.

Click **Image > Attributes....**

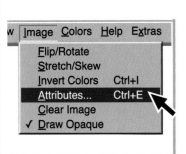

w | Image Colors Help Extras
- Flip/Rotate
- Stretch/Skew
- Invert Colors   Ctrl+I
- Attributes...   Ctrl+E
- Clear Image
- ✓ Draw Opaque

D3 Size and transparency

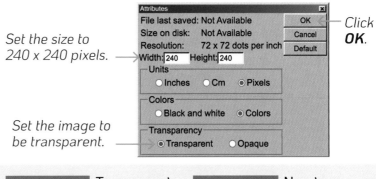

Set the size to 240 x 240 pixels.

Set the image to be transparent.

Attributes   ✕
File last saved: Not Available | OK | — *Click OK.*
Size on disk: Not Available | Cancel |
Resolution: 72 x 72 dots per inch | Default |
Width: 240   Height: 240
┌Units─────────────────────────┐
│ ○ Inches   ○ Cm   ● Pixels   │
└──────────────────────────────┘
┌Colors────────────────────────┐
│ ○ Black and white   ● Colors │
└──────────────────────────────┘
┌Transparency──────────────────┐
│ ● Transparent   ○ Opaque   │
└──────────────────────────────┘

Transparent images will look like this.

Non-transparent (opaque) images have a white background.

Clear the image

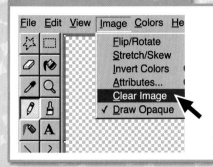

Click **Image** >
Clear Image.

The background of your drawing space should have a grey chequerboard pattern if it is set to be transparent.

05 Start drawing

Use the tools to draw your image. You will need the **Brush** and **Fill** tools.
If you make a mistake, click **Edit** > **Undo**.

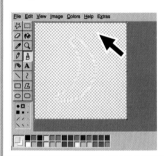  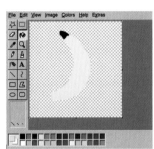 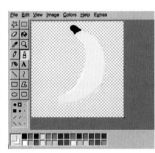

06 Save/Download

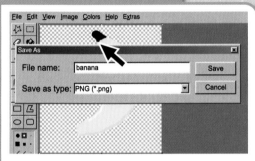

Click **File** > **Save** and type in a file name for your image.

Click **Save** to download/save your file.

07 Save/Download

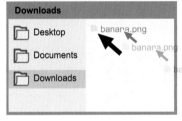 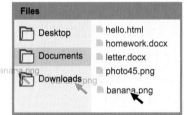

Drag the downloaded file from your Downloads folder into your Documents folder. It needs to be in the same folder that you use for saving your HTML files.

(If you used the Windows program it may already be there.)

08 Add to your code

Find the **img** tag in your code and change the **src** attribute.

```
<img id='food' src='banana.png'>
```
Set this to the file name of your picture.

Save your file and **Refresh** your browser.

Finding Bugs

When you are typing in code it's very easy to make mistakes. Even experienced coders make many mistakes every day. It is part of the learning process, and mistakes can often lead to something useful. Experimentation will help you learn and come up with new ideas.

There's no point getting frustrated about bugs and errors. The important thing is learning how to fix them and learning from your mistakes. Here are some top tips!

Step by step

The projects in this book are designed for you to work **one step at a time**. After you have completed one section, the steps tell you to save, refresh and test your code. Make sure you **fix any errors before moving on** to the next section or it will be very hard to work out what is wrong.

Look carefully at the line numbers when you start a new step.

```
10 <script>
11     balloon.addEv
12     var score=0
```

You need to move your cursor to the start of line 10 and press **Enter** to make some space for the new line 10.

Match line numbers

Book   *Your code*

Look at the start of line 1 in the book and compare it with your line 1. If it's the same, move on to line 2. Skim through all your code this way until you find a difference.

*In the example here, **lines 3 and 4** have not been typed correctly.*

Colour patterns

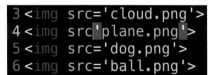

```
3 <img src='cloud.png'>
4 <img src'plane.png'>
5 <img src='dog.png'>
6 <img src='ball.png'>
```

The text editor automatically highlights many errors with colours.

*In the example here, **line 4** is coloured very differently. Look carefully to see which symbol is there in lines 3, 5 and 6, but missing in line 4!*

Spelling

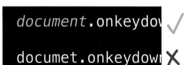

```
document.onkeydow  ✓
documet.onkeydow   ✗
```

Spelling really matters in coding. JavaScript is fussier than the fussiest teacher you will ever have! If it's spelt wrong, it simply won't work. Fortunately, many commands change colour to show they are correct — look for the clues!

Capitals and lowercase

The correct case matters in nearly all of the code in this book. Lots of JavaScript commands are typed in **camelCase**. Most coding languages don't let you type a space within a function name, so coders use capital letters to start each word in a function name.
Check capital and lowercase letters carefully!

mainLoop clearRect drawImage ✓

mainloop clearRECT Drawimage ✗

It is called camelCase because typing in camelCase looks like a camel with lots of humps!

Brackets

There are four different sorts of brackets in HTML and JavaScript — and they all need to be matched carefully! If there are missing symbols, you may get something called a **syntax** error.

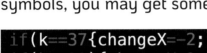

```
if(k==37{changeX=-2;}
if(k==39){changeX=2;}
```

The colours are telling us there is something missing — maybe you can spot it?

If you can't find the error, try looking in the **Developer Console**.

⊗ Uncaught mycode.html:6
SyntaxError: Unexpected
token '{' ←

It has spotted the error and tells you it didn't expect this '{'. You can then see it should be a ')' bracket.

See page 31 for help using the Developer Console.

HTML colour names

There are 140 HTML colour names. They need to be **spelt correctly** for your code to work.

⟳ maxw.com/col
DeepPink
MediumVioletRed
PaleVioletRed
Coral
Tomato
OrangeRed
DarkOrange
Orange
Gold
Yellow

Go to **maxw.com/col** for a complete list of all 140.

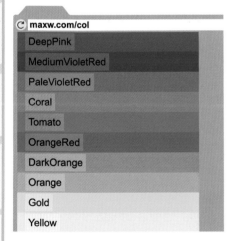

Skim up and down through your code to look for things that look out of place – things that don't fit a pattern.

RGB COLOUR CODES

HTML can actually show over 16 million different colour shades!

To get these shades you need to use **hexadecimal colour codes**. Hexadecimal means base 16, so numbers are counted from 0 to 9 then A, B, C, D, E and F.

The codes work by mixing together Red, Green and Blue light — that's why they are called RGB colour codes.

Colour codes start with #. You can replace the colour words with codes in the projects in this book.

```
background-color:gold;
```

```
background-color:#aa6655;
```

#ffffff
#e6f5ff
#ccebff
#b3e0ff
#99d6ff
#80ccff
#66c2ff
#4db8ff
#33adff
#1aa3ff
#0099ff
#008ae6

Search for "RGB colours" to find out more!

Commands
JavaScript & HTML

HTML CODE	MEANING
`<html>` `</html>`	The start and end of some HTML code.
`<!doctype html>`	Tells the browser this page will be written in HTML.
`<audio>` `</audio>`	Add a sound file to the document. Set the address of the sound with the **src** attribute.
`<canvas>` `</canvas>`	Insert a **canvas** element in the document.
`<div>` `</div>`	Add a **div** element to the page.
`<h1>` `</h1>`	Add a **large heading** to the document.
`<img>`	Put an **image file** onto the page. The address of the picture is set with the **src** attribute.
`<script>` `</script>`	The start and the end of some JavaScript.
`<style>` `</style>`	Add a **style** section to a document.

STYLE CODE	MEANING
`position:absolute;`	This means an element will be positioned with coordinates.
`width:100px;`	Set the width of an element to 100 pixels.
`height:50px;`	Set the height of an element to 50 pixels.
`background-color:red;`	Make the background of an element red.
`border-radius:20px;`	Round the corner of an element by 20 pixels.
`style.left='200px';`	Position an element 200 pixels from the left.
`style.top='150px';`	Position an element 150 pixels from the top.
	Style code is part of another language called CSS. This stands for Cascading Style Sheets.

JAVASCRIPT EVENTS	MEANING
`document.onmousemove=myFunction;`	Run a function called **myFunction** when the mouse is moved.
`document.onkeydown=myFunction;`	When a key is pressed, run a function called **myFunction**.

JAVASCRIPT CODE	MEANING
`alert('Hello!');`	Show a message saying 'Hello!'.
`clearInterval(t);`	Stop a timer called **t**.
`setInterval(main,500);`	Start a timer that will run a function called **main** every half second.
`function mainLoop(){` `}`	Define (make) a function called **mainLoop**. The code inside the curly brackets will be run whenever the **mainLoop()** function is run.
`Math.abs(n);`	This function will return a positive version of the value **n**. Whether **n** is 5 or -5, it will still return 5.
`Math.random()*100;`	This code will return a random number between 0 and 100.
`style.top='150px';`	Position an element 150 pixels from the top.
`var x=100;`	This will declare (create) a variable called **x** with a value of 100.
`var y=[0,100,200];`	Create an array of three numbers, **y[0]**=0, **y[1]**=100 and **y[2]**=200.
`if(x>200)x=200;`	An **if** statement runs some code if the condition inside the brackets is true.
`localStorage.setItem(hs,20);`	Make a semi-permanent variable in the browser called **hs**, and give it a value of 20.
`localStorage.getItem(hs);`	Find out the value of the browser variable called **hs**.
`soundName.play();`	Start playing an audio element named **soundName**.
`soundName.currentTime=0;`	Rewind an audio element to 0 milliseconds.

CANVAS CODE	MEANING
`var ctx=c.getContext('2d');`	Find the canvas element called **c** and link it to a variable called **ctx**. (This is called **getting its context**.)
`ctx.clearRect(0,0,200,150);`	Erase a rectangular area 200 pixels by 150 pixels, starting at the coordinates (0,0).
`ctx.fillRect(10,10,80,120);`	Colour in a rectangular area 80 x 120 pixels, starting at the coordinates (10,10).
`ctx.strokeRect(10,10,40,80);`	Draw a rectangular outline 40 x 80 pixels, starting at the coordinates (10,10).
`ctx.strokeStyle='blue';`	Make the next line drawn on the canvas blue.
`ctx.fillStyle='red';`	Fill in all the shapes drawn on the canvas in red.
`ctx.getImageData(x,y,1,1);`	Find out the colour on the canvas at coordinates (x,y).
`ctx.font='30px Arial';`	Set the font style of text on the canvas.
`ctx.fillText('Hi',50,20);`	Draw text on the canvas at coordinates (50,20).

Glossary

Algorithm A set of rules or steps to make a game or program work.

Array A special sort of variable — more like a list — that can store multiple values.

Browser A program that shows web pages — for example, Chrome, Firefox or Edge.

Bug A mistake or error in a program that stops it running correctly.

Code A series of commands or instructions.

Command An instruction or piece of code that tells the computer to do something.

Coordinates The position of an image on the screen, set by X and Y values.

CSS (Cascading Style Sheets) The language used to set the style of things in an HTML page or document.

Developer Console A special part of a browser used to track errors and bugs in a web page.

Document A web page or HTML file.

Element An image, div, heading or other object added to an HTML page.

Event Something such as a mouse click or key press that happens while code is running.

Function One or more lines of code combined together to carry out a particular task.

HTML The language used to add elements to a web page.

JavaScript The language used to make things happen in a web page.

Listener Some code that listens (waits) until an event like a key press happens.

Milliseconds 1/1000th of a second. There are 500 milliseconds in half a second.

Pixel One of the millions of tiny dots on a computer screen, combined together to show text, graphics or videos.

Random A number that cannot be guessed or predicted.

Refresh To load a web page again so that any changes can be seen.

Right-click Clicking the right-hand mouse button on part of the screen.

Syntax The way words and symbols are arranged to make code.

Text Editor A program used to type code in.

Variable A number or piece of information that can change while a program is running, such as the score in a game.